IRELAND

IRELAND

INTRODUCTION BY MICHEÁL MAC LIAMMÓIR

PHOTOGRAPHS BY EDWIN SMITH

NOTES ON THE PLATES BY OLIVE COOK

WEATHERVANE BOOKS · NEW YORK

Copyright © MCMLXVI by Thames and Hudson Ltd
Library of Congress Catalog Card Number: 66-21196
All rights reserved.
This edition is published by Weathervane Books
a division of Imprint Society, Inc. Distributed by Crown Publishers, Inc.
by arrangement with Thames and Hudson Limited
Text printed in Great Britain by the Camelot Press Ltd Southampton
Color plates printed in Great Britain by Cheney & Sons Ltd, Banbury
Photogravure Plates originated by Ets Braun et Cie Mulhouse France
and printed by Heraclio Fournier, S.A., Vitoria, Spain.

CONTENTS

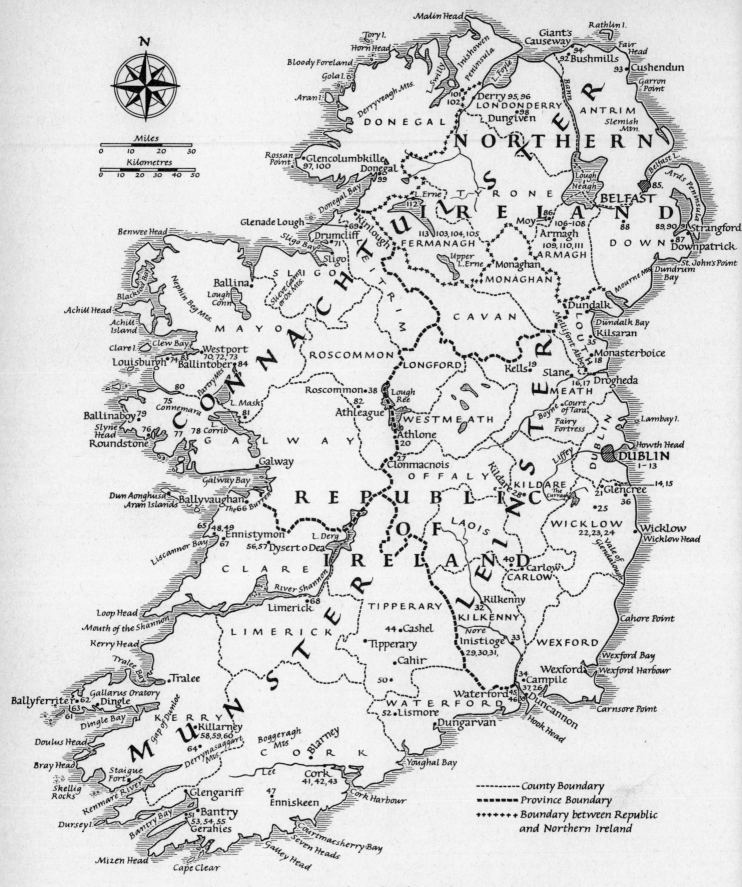

The numbers on the map refer to the Plates and corresponding Notes

IRELAND, IT HAS BEEN SAID, is a land of endless enchantments or as narrow as a pig's back. It all depends on the way you happen to be feeling about it at the moment. The enchantments, apart from sudden orgies of wild beauty among mountains and lakes and lake-islands, are often intangible as a dream: the narrowness of the pig's back can have, at countless moments of despair, the claustrophobic reality of a nightmare, and this may be why many of the people, generally of a natural cheerfulness of disposition, are so often inclined to run away from their country or to die for her. Both these ingrown habits are, of course, methods of escape from an obsession; no country in the world, having produced so little on her own soil, is more absorbed by her own image; no people in the world more bemused by their own reflection in the glass; no nation less interested in the doings or the destinies of other nations; and for these shortcomings, if they are admitted to exist at all, there will always be a host of voluble excuses.

Ah for God's sake, look at our history!

God and history indeed are always ready to the hand, still more so to the lips, and it is interesting to note that geography is seldom resorted to as a means of explaining Irish introversion. For with the exception it may be of Malta and of Iceland, no European island lies in so lamentable and hostile a solitude as Ireland, who has no neighbour on her right hand but her conqueror, and nothing at all on her left but the desolate ocean, not one dry step until you get to America. And America, even after its discovery, must have seemed, for many centuries of sailing-ships, beyond the edge of the known world. In fact, while that world was still believed to be a flat surface over whose edge even a bishop might fall – this must have added a sense of danger to the distance – to be precise, in the year 1169, just one hundred and three years after the Normans had raped and finally (and most properly) married the Saxon colonists of Britain and created from the ceremony a most efficient nation calling itself English, that same new nation, armed to its bland and smiling teeth with ambition, made the first incisive steps in the conquest of Ireland. And by the time that Elizabeth the First ascended the throne the conquest had become wellnigh complete.

It was an interesting period for Irish literature, the one form of art that, in spite of the perpetual wars – still, after four centuries, ravaging the country – struggled for expression. An obstacle race it was in many ways, for the Irish language itself was proscribed and rendered useless for any practical purposes of life and of literature alike; English had as yet no hold upon the people's daily thought or speech; all there had been in the country of printing presses, together with countless Gaelic manuscripts of poetry and prose, were being destroyed; and for a long while the name of Ireland was not allowed to be mentioned in any story, ballad or song. As the country herself had been, since the earliest days of the English invasion, the chief topic of her literature, the poets, the ballad-makers and the tellers of tales took the age-long refuge of the apron-strings, and the goddesses of mythological faith were invoked. Had not Ireland received her three most ancient names from three goddesses of pagan days? They were Éire, Fódla, and Banba, and now, some two thousand years later, the goddesses reappeared in a new guise. Caitlín ní Uallacháin (pronounced, and often wrongly spelt, as Cathleen Ní Houlihaun), Róisín Dubh – the Little Black Rose, Síle ní Ghadhra and many other titles were found for the country whose own name – Éire in the old language, Ireland in the new – was not to be breathed, and a queer series of images formed in the popular mind moulded by poetical fancy: a royal, restive, gorgeous, war-bedraggled captive: a martyred rose-like virgin crowned with stars: a poor old woman – the Sean-Bhean

1 THE METAL FOOT BRIDGE FROM NOONAN'S SHIRT FACTORY, DUBLIN

The graceful iron structure over the Liffey between Grattan and O'Connell Bridges was built as Wellington Bridge in 1816 and is now commonly known as the Metal Bridge. Noonan's Shirt Factory, from the rusticated arch of which the photograph was taken, was once the Merchants' Hall, built by Frederick Darley in 1821. The splendid colouring of the bars, shops and warehouses on the quays provides a foretaste of one of the most striking features of Irish country towns, the uninhibited use of vivid, contrasting washes on every façade.

bhocht of many a Jacobean rhapsody – dragging her tattered cloak about her as she trudged over the hills and down the wet, winding roads, the noise of bird-song or the thunder of battle forever sounding in the air about her head.

The country, in fact, appeared in many incarnations, as indeed she does to this day, according to the eyes of the seer. Her greatest English-speaking poet, William Butler Yeats, celebrates her as the traditional penurious Old Woman who becomes, as soon as she has found the willing sacrifice she seeks, a beautiful young girl with 'the walk of a queen'; her greatest inventor in English prose, James Joyce, refers to her as the 'old sow who eats her own farrow'.

It all depends, as I have suggested, on the way you happen to be feeling about her at the moment; for never has an apparently insignificant country, whose very existence seems unknown even to post-offices in many otherwise well-informed places, appeared in so many guises or created such tempests of love and hatred, so much worship and so much contempt among its own people, or those interested strangers who belong, ironically enough, almost exclusively to the English-speaking world.

Even in these, the innocence of any knowledge of her history, her true personality, among the most demonstrative enthusiasts, is astonishing. In America, for example, the annual hysteria of St Patrick's Day, the Irish national festival, fills the streets from

II THE VIRGIN AND CHILD PAGE FROM THE BOOK OF KELLS

The famous illuminated manuscript of the Four Gospels, from which this full-page illustration is taken, is named after the monastery of St Columba at Kells, Co. Meath (*see also* plate 19). It was probably written and illumi- nated at Iona at the beginning of the 9th century and brought to Kells in a still-unfinished state, when the Abbot of Iona fled with his monks to Kells to escape the Norse invaders. The manuscript remained at Kells until 1653, was then sent to Dublin, and ten years later was given to Trinity College (where it remains), probably by Henry Jones, Bishop of Meath. The style of this extraordinary painting shows affinities with Merovingian illumina- tions and with Northumbrian manuscript pages, in particular with those of the Lindisfarne Gospels, which belong to a century earlier. The effect is emphatically abstract despite the subject, so great is the obsession with in- tricate interlacings, coilings and windings, spirals, knot patterns, fret and step motifs, which conspire to make the figures part of one big mosaic of ornament, barbaric in its over-abundance and yet wholly superhuman, wholly imperturbable. The linear design to which the Virgin and Her dress have been reduced immediately recalls the schematic images of the Earth Mother goddess at New Grange (*see* plate 16).
Reproduced by permission of the Board of Trinity College, Dublin.

morning till night of the 17th of March with bands and banners, shamrocks and shillelaghs, drums and drummers, young ladies in saffron kilts, young gentlemen in emerald-coloured trousers and plastic top hats of the same colour. It is a day when everyone discovers an Irish grandmother in his family and blithely wishes everyone else, regardless of the time of day, 'the Top o' the Morning' – a phrase unknown in Ireland at any hour at all; a day when the uninitiated is given the strangest impression of a country in whose existence, outside a Walt Disney cartoon, no one could believe for a moment. It is a synthetic nursery world of 'leprechauns' (the *lioprachán* is a fairy shoemaker), bottles of whiskey, knee-breeches, blackthorn clubs called shillelaghs, gilt harps, green beer, and a facetious form of banter called Blarney (a place in Cork which rhymes with Killarney in Kerry and is useful in jocular or lachrymose songs). In fact, from all that is said or believed in America about the Irish, and there is a good deal, you would get the impression that they were a collection of high-spirited half-wits who, when not engaged in fighting, praying, drinking whiskey, or paying you compliments (that is part of the Blarney), spend most of their time dancing jigs and seeing leprechauns. In this fantasy the female population are known as 'colleens' (from *cailín*, a young girl); all of them are lovely youthful creatures or lovable doting hags. That ubiquitous and ominously vigorous figure of real life in Ireland, the middle-aged matron, is unknown to this school of trans-Atlantic imagery. Well then, the 'colleens' occasionally play the harp, pausing now and then to laugh merrily as they milk a cow or two, knee-deep in king-size shamrocks – pigs are seldom mentioned in America: it is the English tradition in which they play so large a part – and over all, the b'hoys and the colleens and the cows alike, the same sweet rain streams softly down, lending to the entire landscape that curious virulent green that is reflected in the clothes they wear and the drinks they consume.

Now, uninventive as the Irish may be, they have given more to the world than whiskey, the harp, and the green of the shamrock. They have given an inexplicably neglected mythology, unsurpassed in wildness and beauty by any but that of Greece; a literature in two languages; a unique style of ornament in bronze and gold and stone; forms of verse and rhyme; various schools of religious and mystical thought; a few saints and a few scholars (though fewer, it may be, than is generally claimed); a few musical forms; and a host of poets, wits and writers of comedy. (They also, it is said, invented trousers and the safety-pin, which seems unlikely but may be true.)

Nor is the country that bore these men and these things of that monotonous, all-pervading greenness the enthusiasts who have never seen it would have you believe.

12

There is in Irish mythology a region in the depths of the Land of the Young, the Celtic Valhalla, that is known as *Ioldathach*, the Many Coloured Land, and the visible Ireland in which we live and work and talk with our friends seems, at times, to be but the reflection of that visionary place. I am writing these words in a little town in Connemara, and when I look out of the window I see, above the thatched and slated roofs, April driving wild, dappled clouds across the sky, brightening or darkening the waters of a score of still, small lakes and running streams, alternately veiling and revealing the faint mountains far away, filling at one moment the grey of the craggy hillside with shadow or blurring the gold furze-blossom with light. The rainbow's arc is poised above thin, floating vapours, a flight of swallows passes, a black-and-white cat, misleadingly demure, sits at the door of a house whose walls are daubed with light blue. And everywhere the airs are coloured, multitudinous and ever-changing, as subtle and fleeting as the noise of water running among stones. The green, of course, is everywhere, but for the most part you will find it in brief and unexpected moments of intensity: in a handful of little fields huddled between low, ragged walls of loose stones that appear at times in the tricky light like strings of broken pearls; in ridges of coarse grass by the road-side; in rings and knolls that grow over the raths, the burial places of the ancients – it is, I think, never the predominant note, even in the fat pasture-lands of Meath or Dublin. Still less is it all-pervading in those regions in the west or south where, in my eyes, the country reveals her ultimate secrets among rocks and mountains and glens and the dense purplish-brown of bogs riddled with glittering water and darkened by thorn-trees twisted by the Atlantic winds. Here, if there be any basic colour note at all, it is silver or grey or gold, according to the weather's capricious fancy, and on certain rare summer evenings, unless you are staring directly into the west in search of some fiery magic, the earth and the sky and the water slowly wrap themselves in a mantle of blue so dimly profound you feel you could hold it in your arms.

The first race said by ancient legend to have appeared in Ireland – they were, it is believed, invaders, and who was there before them is unknown – were the *Fir Bolg*, which means literally (and oddly) 'Bag-Men'. One imagines them to have been what later legend, known to us as history, has agreed to call the Iberian Celts, and their Mediterranean ancestry is clear in their descendants to this day, not in Ireland alone, but in south-western England, in Wales and in the Scottish Highlands. They were, and are, for the most part of small to medium height, wiry, swift-moving, dark-haired and dark-eyed, and their presence in these far-away islands is too ubiquitous to be accounted for by the popular romantic notions about the Spanish Armada, or even by the more sophisticated theories about the trading years between northern Spain and Galway, a commercial relationship that undoubtedly existed from the 14th to the 17th century. If the Spanish navy or the Spanish merchants are really responsible for the physiognomy of so many dwellers in the westerly regions of these islands, named British by the ruling classes, where are the Spanish names? Must we believe that so many virtuous maidens of Devon, Cornwall, Wales, western Scotland, above all of Ireland, were so lavishly indiscriminate with their favours that, with the help of their southern visitors – a few commercial gentlemen from Bilbao, a handful of shipwrecked seamen (however able-bodied) from His Most Catholic Majesty's Armada – that together they could transform the inhabitants of a cluster of northern sea-coasts into their own likeness? And in such large numbers? For in Ireland alone, the number of men and women of Mediterranean features, colouring and temper is, in Ireland's latitude, astonishing.

The *Fir Bolg* were invaded by a second race, history continues; a tall fair-skinned people with tawny red hair and greenish eyes who called themselves the *Tuatha Dé Dánaan*, the Tribes of the Goddess Dana. They were mystically inclined and brought with them a complicated form of nature-worship, the belief in reincarnation, priests and magicians who were known as Druids, and a host of gods and goddesses reduced by the later faith of Christianity to a fantastic capricious race of small invisible beings called the Faeries, who are widely believed in to this day. Once more the title of these red-headed people was changed by later scholars who called them Picts, and the thought has occasionally struck me that they may well be the origin of that whimsical little English phantom known as the Pixie. At any rate, like so many religious sects, the *Tuatha Dé Dánaan* (or Picts) possessed a curious vein of social superiority. They despised the poor *Fir Bolg* and made them into slaves, but if ever they decided to exterminate them they must either have failed or changed their minds, because they, with their dark colouring, their clear-cut features, are still, in our own 20th century, here, there and everywhere, as numerous as the redheads themselves, if not more so. These, in turn, were tyrannized over by a third invasion who were, and still are, known as the Gaels, and who were said – it was almost certainly themselves who said it – to be 'valiant, voluble, laughing and war-like: brown-haired and bright-eyed, skilled in the arts of peace and battle alike'. They brought with them a strikingly logical system of government, a High-King with several smaller Kings under him; a considerable skill in the

14

fashioning of gold and silver and bronze; a tireless gift of the gab; and an accompany-
ing passion for poetry, story-telling, drinking, hunting, fighting, feasting, and running off with each other's husbands and wives.

The Gaels, in turn, despised both the Iberians and the Picts: the former, we are told,
were given the heaviest and most menial of labours, and the latter, although they were
held in a certain superstitious awe – were they not adepts in the magical arts? – were
forced to live in underground raths and caves, to dress in green 'like the common
grass', and to be always indoors in their subterranean homes after the fall of twilight;
nor were they allowed to emerge until the sun had risen.

Did they perhaps steal out of their grassy mounds and caves in the earth on clear
summer nights to dance the sacred dances of their faith under the boughs of hawthorn
and blossoming rowan? And with their pale faces, gleaming eyes and red hair stream-
ing on the wind over their green dresses, what mythologies might they not have en-
gendered in the mind of some dark-eyed Iberian huddled half-awake in his sheepskin
blanket by the roadside; of some Gaelic housewife standing at the door of her house,
peering over the rocky hillside for a sight of her man and her sons coming home from
the woods?

With the passing of the years, of course, the three early races were gradually merged –
much as the Saxons and the Normans at a later date in England were merged – and
the strongest among them being the Gaels, they gave their name to all the peoples of
Ireland although they were, in fact, no more completely Gaelic than the peoples of
what is known as Great Britain are, in fact, completely British. St Patrick, who was
probably a Frenchman, though some claim him for Wales, had been brought as a
child to Ireland where, as a slave, he was set to watch sheep on a northern mountain
called Sliabh Mis (pronounced, and sometimes written, as Slieve Mish). On that
mountainside, in his master's house, and among the surrounding plains, he watched
not only sheep, but many other things, and a passion to change much of what he saw
must already have been smouldering in his breast when, as a youth, having escaped
from bondage, he went back to the Continent where he became a theological student
of considerable brilliance. After some years at Avignon he was ordained at Rome, and
returned in the prime of his manhood and the flower of his achievement to the island
that had enslaved him as a boy, and for which he had preserved, paradoxically enough,
an unchanging affection. He brought with him a handful of Christian monks, an
iron-like will, a great deal of knowledge of humanity as well as of theological principle,
both Christian and pagan, an inordinate passion for argument – he once even argued

with an angel, and won – and an unshakable conviction that he could convert the Irish from their faith in the Druids and the Priests of the Sun to his own religious beliefs. This he proceeded to do, and with such rapid success that, during his own lifetime, more than three-quarters of the people became converts and were baptized as Christians. Even the Druids, those powerful masters of the mysteries, were of little use against him: for every magical feat they performed, Patrick would answer with a Christian miracle, providing the Court of Tara with a series of breath-taking feats of supernatural power, causing the nobles to burst into applause and the High-King Laoire himself to be baptized. The Queen and the courtiers rapidly followed his example and this undoubtedly made a profound impression on the more snobbish portions of the population that always, one imagines, looked to the royal seat of Tara for a lead in matters of worldly or celestial decision.

And so the era of early Christianity began: its finest remaining works in stone and bronze and gold were mostly miniatures. There are, in many museums, chalices, cups, goblets, croziers and crucifixes, some superbly illuminated manuscripts and many elaborate collars, diadems, bracelets and other articles of personal attire; and it is strange to note the sumptuous quality of these things and to compare it to the scarcity of the architectural remains of Ireland's glory during those ages described in other European countries as Dark. To be sure, there is, in the County Tipperary, Cashel, a fantastically lovely monument of the 10th and 12th centuries, there is the incomparable Clonmacnois in the County Offaly, as well as numerous small churches and monkish cells, and the famous Round Towers still point ambiguously to the skies here, there and everywhere. But Tara of the Kings is grass, and of the castles of the lesser Kings and Princes hardly a stone remains. The explanation is that these edifices were not made with stones at all: the ancient Irish, both pagan and Christians, it is said, like the Egyptians, constructed their dwelling places of wood: according to old tradition they loved roofs that were thatched with straw and turf-sods and rushes and sometimes 'with the feathers of the eagle and the hawk', and the Irish climate would not be slow in the destruction of such things. The ecclesiastics, who were among the privileged classes, as the Druids and the Poets had been before them, seem to have been very busy men, and among many more sedentary occupations they made frequent trips abroad, where they built so many churches and converted so many of the heathen that their artless Continental followers took to calling Ireland 'The Island of Saints and Scholars'. This pretty title is still extant, and there are quite a lot of Irish people who, having lived in the country all their lives and knowing, presumably, something about it, will earnestly

16

quote the phrase to this day (especially if foreigners are present) without being struck dead by lightning on the spot.

Nations always appear to me to be individuals in slow motion, if you see what I mean: a nation, like a man, passes through Shakespeare's seven ages of development, from the abandoned puling and puking of babyhood to the annihilation of old age and of death, though the process in the nation is, naturally enough, more gradual. Yet, to my mind, there is a strange exception to the rule: an individual man, producing nothing outside his own personality, creates about him little impact on all but a few intimate friends whose hearts he may touch and whose minds he probably bores to melancholy toleration: a nation producing but little becomes, through a subtle alchemical process, more and more vivid in the imagination of the interested foreign spectators. The mere fact of having made so small an impression on world history adds to the aura that surrounds the national character a certain defiant, insolent fire. The Gypsies are a case in point: the most vivid, it may be, of all cases. The Poles, the Hungarians, the Swiss and the Irish are others. It would be absurd to say of these that any among them had not produced, from time to time, men of outstanding genius, contributions of the highest distinction to other civilizations, to other schools of expression, but if you compare them to, say, Greece, Italy, France, England and Germany, it will be obvious that they have made no collective impact at all on European tradition. It may be that they lack the yeasty assertiveness that is a part of the flair for organization, the pride in concerted action, the delight of belonging to some great image that one has helped to create, and that has grown greater than oneself. Certainly, when one thinks of Greece, of Italy, of France, of England, or of Germany, one thinks of their monuments; in conjuring up Ireland to the mind's eye, one thinks first of mountain and lake and bogland, secondly of people.

Indeed, there is little else to consider. Ireland, who bore Cúchulainn, Fionn mac Cumhaill and Brian Ború, has had no Alexander or Caesar or Napoleon. She brought forth Déirdre and Maebh, but no Helen of Troy and no Joan of Arc. She gave us Eoghan ó Súilleabháin but no Dante; Erigéna but no Plato; Raftery but no Villon; Swift and Yeats and Wilde and Shaw, but no Shakespeare and no Goethe. And to ourselves, it may be, it is the world that is lacking in perception, not Ireland in fruitfulness. Certainly it is for tragic historical reasons that she can point to no great city that summarizes her personality: no Venice, Vienna or Versailles, no splendour of Paris or London or Rome to boast of; no Stratford-on-Avon or Bayreuth or Maison

17

de Molière; no works in marble or paint or bronze to compare with those of Leonardo or Michelangelo; no school like the Impressionists of France; no names in psychiatric discovery like Freud or Jung, or in revolutionary influence like Marx or Lenin. Even her mountains are not as high or as physically handsome as Alps or Dolomites, nor her folk-dancing as violently provocative as that of Spain. The little task of subtraction could continue forever and would take nothing away from her indescribable magic, any more than it could shake for one moment the relaxed self-assurance of the simplest, shyest and most uninstructed of her sons and daughters. They do not feel in the least superior, or pompous, or proud; certainly they do not feel humble or bowed-down. Nor do they give a damn about their own Swifts and Yeatses: they simply feel grand! Gorgeous they feel they are, and, in their own words, no more about it.

This, doubtless, is what gives to them, in their own eyes and in the eyes of strangers, one of their most endearing qualities: they are, for the most part, restful. Relaxed and restful. That is the secret of what strangers call Irish charm. They are restful. Almost alone, I think, in Northern Europe, they do not spend their time in counting how many are the stairs, or windows, or yards, or revolutions of the wheel, or whatever it may be; they seldom worry you by pressing food on you, or making quite certain that you really *are* seated comfortably; they seldom calculate time and money, one eye forever on the future; they are seldom obsessed by factual details: in a word, they seldom fuss. This, of course, carries its own disadvantages. The national vice, I think, is a profound indifference to wellnigh all things, there is a widespread passion for procrastination, and the reputation for being unreliable, scatty and forgetful is not wholly without

III THE WATERFALL, POWERSCOURT, CO. WICKLOW

The scene of the waterfall in the Powerscourt Demesne, the Dargle valley, presents the strongest possible contrast to the landscape garden in front of the house (*see* plate 15), not only in its extreme wildness, but in the narrowness of its confines. The water falls, with a boom loud enough to stun a man, into a glade hemmed in by mountain steeps, and in this constricted place the wind reaches such a pitch of fury that it is scarcely possible to stand. In such an atmosphere the impact of this most spectacular of cataracts is more than visual: it seems to hit the head and breast like a severe electric shock. The water slides with awesome force, smooth as molten lead, over the brow of an immense precipice caught between two close walls of rock; then, suddenly released, it falls four hundred feet in one glistening sheet of snowy white, crashing in a seething, smoking cloud into a dark pool of tremendous depth.

foundation. Like the Italians, they can be brilliant in an emergency, but the emergency has to arise before they dream of blowing the fire to flame; although they enjoy life in their own fashion, disaster and the possibility of death must come close before the conscious will to live is aroused.

Do I exaggerate? Probably. But I do not invent. I have lived among my own people for far the greater part of my life and share in many of their ways, and almost all of their weaknesses but a few (horse-racing, hunting, gambling and fishing having no charm for me), and the few years I have spent in England, France, Spain and elsewhere have merely freshened observation. It is extraordinary, if one never lives away from one's own country at all, how much of its gold and dross can pass unnoticed. What man living continually in the shadow of the Parthenon, or in the depths of a slum, will be completely aware of either? And in Ireland, as in other places, one meets, among people and things alike, both Parthenon and slum everywhere and at any moment of the night or day.

I said something just now about horse-racing, hunting, fishing and gambling having no charms for me, and I am sad when I think over the many things to whose delights I am blind and deaf. It is because of this, it may be, that I feel compelled to say now that Ireland breeds superb horses whose characters, I am told, are deeply endearing when you get to know them: they are paraded on two separate and sensational weeks, every spring and every summer, in Dublin's Horse Shows, where they behave, in the

IV DONKEY AND FLAT CART, ENNISTYMON, CO. CLARE

Before the 19th century the spoked wheel was reserved for the carriages of
the rich. It was then adopted for farm carts, having been introduced into
Ulster from Scotland. The so-called flat cart with projecting trams was able
to take far greater loads than the wheel-car with its solid wheels (see plate
and note 59), though it was not suitable for work in rough fields and bogs.
The flat cart consists of little more than a slatted platform without fixed
sides and ends. It can be fitted with a variety of sides for different purposes.
Here a single open side has been attached to support the milk churns. The
woodwork of flat carts is usually brightly painted. Such carts are now found
chiefly in the west of Ireland, where they are commonly used for hawking.

V SHOP FRONTS, ENNISTYMON, CO. CLARE

The rich colours which enliven Irish country towns, together with the old-
fashioned shop fronts, give the streets the robust character of Pollock Toy
Theatre prints.

main, with admirable decorum and a gracefully exhibitionist consciousness of their own glossy charms. I should add that the hunting is ideal, if strenuous, which after all is only to be expected – most invigorating too if you don't happen to be a fox; that gambling is widespread and wildly encouraged; and that the rivers Shannon, Lee and Boyne are as full of salmon as are the lakes and streams of trout and other delicacies. About the hunting, shooting and fishing I, like many other inconsistent people, am given to humanitarian qualms until the victims of these manly pastimes appear on the table, for what could be better than a pheasant, unless it be a *civet de lièvre* or a *canard sauvage aux cerises* or even a *darne de saumon*?

The 'ordinary' people of Ireland, by the way, have a curious distaste for fish: they are expected, naturally enough, to eat it on Fridays and other days of abstinence, which (also naturally enough) annoys them; for Irish people are irresistibly repelled by anything that is expected of them – they never, in their hearts, thought much of Lord Nelson – and they vent their annoyance by cooking almost all fish extremely badly.

They even despise those magnificent lobsters that float round the coast in lapis-lazuli luxuriance. In my younger days they frequently flung them back into the sea and despised those people who ate them; nowadays they sometimes banish them to England in exchange for gold.

There is in Ireland a widespread passion for Sport (once more I am blind and deaf), and Football, Boxing and *Iomáint*, or Hurling, are all popular. Hurling is the national game and is played with balls and *maidí iomána*, or *camáin* (hurling sticks), by males (in shorts) and with *camógaí* (a modified version of the hurling stick) by females (in saffron-coloured kilts). It is very noble and swift and exciting, even if you know nothing at all about it; it is probably, indeed almost certainly, dangerous (one hears of dreadful effects on family life) and is accompanied by wild cries of encouragement or the reverse, and frequently followed by savagely impressionistic photographs in the newspapers and by vivacious close-ups on television.

So that really, you see, there is something to appeal to almost every taste in Ireland.

Children all over the world, if surrounded by reasonably loving care, are born with the comfortable conviction that life is a picnic to which they are expected to contribute nothing at all but the fascination of their presence and the fun they themselves get out of it. Not for them to organize the meeting place, the selected spot, the cold chickens, the buttered rolls, the bottles of wine or the washing up; nor is any rational creature annoyed if they fail to do these things. It is only when they grow older that they realize, often through bitter experience, that life is not like that for any prolonged period; that they find themselves confronted by a wilderness of problems known as responsibilities which, in one way or another, they have to deal with, to overcome, to bend to their will and somehow to set in order, while being careful not to inflict themselves or their fellows with mortal wounds. In Ireland we have an astonishingly large portion of the adult population who never arrive at this depressing conclusion at all, remaining, on the contrary, convinced from cradle to grave that life is a chaotic comedy whose grimmer moments, with a little shuffling, may almost invariably be avoided by the simple expedient of turning away from them, of getting too drunk to remember them, or (more simple still) of walking out on them. And here, lest it be thought that I may have fallen into the fatal and fascinating habit of generalizing about the national characteristics of no matter what country, race or tradition, let me say that I speak in the broadest and most impressionist terms of that section of the community we may as well describe as Average: the individual artist, dictator, priest, politician, or who you will, is almost invariably untypical of his nation. If for any reason at all, then, you want to get rid of the average Irishman, present him with a problem: he will vanish with all the swiftness of a dream. In England, in France, in Spain, if an actor, say, or a secretary, or a domestic servant is wretchedly dissatisfied with his lot there will be one or another result; you will get from him the reaction of sullen service, or you will, sooner or later, hear all about it. The part is too small, the hours are too long, the office is unsatisfactory, the stairs are too many: they will put up with their fate for this or that reason, or they will complain, warn, threaten or give notice: in short, they will suffer and serve in grudging silence or they will make manifest their sad story. In Ireland it is unlikely that you will learn anything at all but what your own sharpened or blunted senses tell you: you will be served and smiled upon for a day, for two, even for three days, and you will then, quietly and unostentatiously, be abandoned. They quite simply will appear no more. If you track the absentee to his, or indeed to her, lair, bent on information, you will be told of other contracts (actors), failing health (clerks), nervous breakdowns (secretaries), or dying relatives (domestics); and these baffling reasons for disappearance, you reflect, may or may not be true: you will never know. All you can be certain of is that they want no more of you, and still more important, that they have no wish to hurt your feelings. That they have done far worse to you than that never occurs to them, because all that really is of interest is the fact that they have successfully avoided something that might disturb what Shaw called their 'dreaming, dreaming, dreaming'. 'No debauchery', he continues, 'that ever coarsened or brutalized an Englishman can take the worth and usefulness out of him like that dreaming.' Shaw goes on to explain how 'an Irishman's imagination never lets him alone, never convinces him, never satisfies him, but it makes him so that he can't deal with it nor handle it nor conquer it, he can only sneer at them that do...'

I agree with him, except that I would not call it imagination. Imagination, as I understand it, is not a prevailing quality of our people; a reverie as of Nirvana has taken its place. The only active form the national imagination has taken lies, for me, in the fact that they have imagined an imagination for themselves: they are as convinced of their imaginative nature as the English are convinced of their love of Fresh Air and Fair Play, and how either nation has arrived at its strange conclusions is, to me, an unfathomable mystery.

What the Irish majority really can do, when not engaged in the favourite pastime of a sort of immobile, pan-faced reverie, is to talk. They will talk with relish, eloquence and grandeur, often about nothing at all, their minds, equally often, far away in some other nothingness. They will also discourse, with or without knowledge, on any subject under the moon. Indeed it may well be that the gift of the gab, undeniably a far more common characteristic among them than among other people of northern Europe, is what has given them their reputation for the imaginative faculty. The gift of the gab combined, it may be, with that curious, electrical, instinctive sensitivity to unseen forces that characterizes many animals – cats, horses and dogs in particular – as well as many human creatures who live in countries where mechanical civilization has not entirely deadened the more delicate senses. It is remarkable how a combination of two qualities will enable a man to masquerade as the possessor of a third which he does not, in fact, possess, and which is of a totally different nature from those to which he may in truth lay claim. A pronounced talent, combined with an inborn self-assurance and eccentricity of behaviour, for example, has often been hailed by an eager and apparently discriminating world as Genius, when in sober truth it is no such thing. A friendly sympathy, accompanied by powerful physical attraction, is daily mistaken by perfectly honest people for Love. Surely then the wellnigh universal Irish characteristic of a natural friendliness, ease and richness of speech, coupled with the more mysterious instinct at which I have hinted, may lend to the individual, and to the race, the illusion of being imaginative.

But the land itself is rich in the stuff of imagination. With all its variety, from the rolling pasture lands of Meath in the east and Tipperary in the south to the plains and bogs of Longford, Ossory and Westmeath, from those deep embowered recesses among woods and running streams and half-forgotten green places in Cork and Waterford and Wicklow with their suggestion of some early 19th-century idyll to the naked stony magnificence of Aran or of Clare, there breathes everywhere a sense of intimacy and wonder; of a suspended, secret, smiling mystery. To wander anywhere beyond the borders of some large or little town until one comes to the lonely places is to feel that everything about one, every stone and tree and bush, every mountain and lake and wave of the sea, is something seen, as it were, in a mirror, or something, it may be, that is but the mask covering the face of a deeper beauty. It is a mood that finds its most complete expression in English perhaps in Yeats's lines:

> *Do our woods and winds and ponds*
> *Cover more quiet woods, more shining winds, more star glimmering ponds?*
> *Is Eden out of time and out of space?*

And one senses this mood at moments even among the traffic of Irish cities and towns, for nowhere is the countryside very far away. You can see the tops of blue mountains from many of the streets of Dublin and Belfast; indeed, were it not for this, Dublin and Belfast would be duller places than they are.

Not that they can claim to any excessive brilliance; Dublin has about it a leisurely, dawdling *désinvolture* and a certain restless consciousness of its own incompleteness that makes it a fine place in which to live and work: it is at once ambitious and lazy, dissipated and pious, elegant and slovenly, thick-headed and witty, friendly and malicious, knowledgeable and naïve, tolerant and ungracious, quizzical and deeply imperceptive. It is also, alas – and I have said this of it somewhere before to the applause and hisses of many friends – cynical without knowledge, blasé without experience. It is, in fact, a city that is half small capital, half provincial town; and but for its superb natural setting between mountain and sea-coast, and for certain lovely 18th-century squares and streets, one wonders at times why so many famous poets, dramatists and wits chose it for their birthplace.

The 18th-century squares and streets, by the way, together with many isolated mansions of equal beauty, are in daily increasing peril at the hands of present-day barbarians who are passionately engaged in demolishing them and causing them to be replaced everywhere by those spine-chilling Halma boards and packing-cases of steel and plate glass mounted on square legs that are making our whole planet, from Limerick to Tokyo, so uniform that indeed architectural depression may well be a part of the reason why so many people have become anxious, as earthly travel – for any purpose but that of business – seems more and more pointless, to remove themselves to the moon.

Yet Dublin, with its peerless natural setting of mountains and forest and coast-line, can still boast of a few man-made objects of pride. It has two universities: Trinity College, designed by Queen Elizabeth the First for the sons of English gentlemen, and kept in rigid seclusion for them and their descendants for many years, and the University College, a young, heroic national gesture housed in an architectural invention of the early 1900s, compassionately screened by flowering cherry trees; it has the fine art galleries, museums and national libraries one would expect of a capital city, the usual hotels and shops and cafés; more theatres than it can regularly fill; more cinemas, it is said, than any other town of its size in the world (these, as a rule, are packed to the roof); film studios, radio and television stations; and it has lately acquired the habit, beloved of taxi-drivers and abhorred by all other members of the population, of one-way streets. The taxi-drivers are splendid people, invariably of the male sex – the lady chauffeur is so far unknown – and their frequently sketchy knowledge of their own city and its suburbs is atoned for by their still more frequent eloquence, their friendly personal interest in you, and their willingness to impart information on any subject at all but the whereabouts of your destination; also by their (to the stranger) incredible indifference about the size of their tips if you happen to be short of change. 'Ah sure you'll see me again, please God', is the usual formula and this, after similar experiences in Paris, London, or New York, has a soothing effect. On the other hand, unlike the drivers of Paris, London or New York, they seem seldom to possess any change themselves and often have to run with astonishing speed for a couple of hundred yards or so, probably under driving rain, until they have plucked the necessary silver and copper from some huckster's shop, returning so dramatically breathless, so drenched and so bravely smiling, that if you have a heart at all you feel you must give them much more than you would have done were they themselves efficiently provided. And it is through such trivialities as this that in Ireland you come to understand the folly of being practical.

In Cork, the serene, the inimitable Cork, the second city of the Republic, the undisputed Queen of the South, the details of daily life – taxi-drivers, bus conductors, offices and shops, restaurant gossip, proletariat eloquence, theatre-going, social activities and so on – are much the same as in the capital. But Cork on the whole is a more harmonious place. Structurally and physically it has a perceptible design, from

26

the early 18th-century houses on the South Mall and the Parade to the placid river-side walks among low wooded hills that are like the hills embroidered on an early Victorian sampler. The 'Sweet Cork' of Father Prout, like the Shandon bells with their odd, nostalgic chime, has an authentic sound on the ear; there is reality in the phrase. For Cork, self-contained, quizzical, audacious, critical, hard-drinking, capricious, contentedly conservative, gaily tranquil, rapid in thought and speech, leisurely in motion, Cork is both sweet and essentially and seriously comedic in the essence of its being. It has a tempo, a shape and a style more apparent than that of the restlessly cerebral, pretentiously casual, quasi-sophisticated, insistently scatterbrained Dublin. It has little of the melancholy refinement of Limerick, where the great river, the medieval towers and castle walls, the 18th-century mansions fade gently into a network of drab poverty, or into a silvery, retrospective feminine resignation, and where the newest shops and hotels have a modernity so staccato in their borrowed American style that you feel that, like Wilde's débutante in *An Ideal Husband*, they are in danger of growing old-fashioned quite suddenly. Cork is nostalgic but it has little of the poignancy of Limerick. Nor has it anything of the tragic mingling of nobility and squalor that lies at the heart of Galway with its dark crumbling castles and broken walls, its rushing river, its desolate Fish Market, its vanished Claddagh, its palaces and hovels, its Gaelic Theatre and Spanish Arch and grass-grown quays, its oddly violent note, its great bay that is guarded on the south by the hills of Clare and its glittering or storm-shrouded Atlantic horizon where the sun dies every evening over the three islands of Aran. Cork, whose essence is neither tragic nor violent, is aesthetically ambitious and harmoniously minded, and has many concerts and crowded evenings of orchestral and chamber music, although it can boast of no annual operatic festival like that of Wexford. It is full of memories, but it has no monument as significant in the story of Irish destiny as Waterford, where in the vast barrack-like Reginald's Tower by the river you may walk in the room where, shipped over from England by Henry II, the Norman knight Strongbow married Aoife, the daughter of an Irish king, and by that marriage closed the door on an era of many centuries and opened the long chapter of the longest resisted occupation that European history has known.

Cork may have none of these things, but it has its annual international film festival, its opera house – a new one, opened in November 1965, the old, beloved, very ugly one having been burned out a few years since – its famous Shandon and Mardyke and Sunday's Well, its Cathedrals to St Mary and to its own St Finbarr; its cheerful hilly streets, steepled churches and fine shops, its Queen's University, its art gallery, its good restaurants and pleasant bosky surroundings of river- and sea-bordered suburbs, its logi-cal, optimistic twist of English and Irish speech, its lengthy list of distinguished sons and daughters who can claim it as their birthplace, and also its large and lovely lunatic-asylum, one of the most striking buildings in the city.

It also has a perpetual eye on the day when, Dublin having been dispossessed, it will take its rightful place as Ireland's first city, and its favourite motto is '*Luimneach a bhí, Baile Átha Cliath atá, Corcaigh a bhéidh*', which means 'Limerick that was, Dublin that is, Cork that shall be'.

Only most Corcagians would put it 'Cork that will be', for with all their nimble-ness in acquiring the English language the Irish people have never solved the mys-teries of 'will' and 'shall'.

Irish is still a living language – and by this I mean a language still naturally alive, not one resurrected like Lazarus from the tomb by miracles or even by injections – though how it has remained so is a mystery.

How widely is it spoken in those barren and beautiful places among mountains and by lonely seas to which it has been driven year by year and where it has found its last refuge? Census figures are available, of course, but they make forlorn reading, for the dwindling of Irish speakers 'from the cradle' still goes on in spite of the desperate efforts made to encourage them to continue their lives in their own tongue, which seems to themselves synonymous with a lonely isolation. The value of that tongue, like the value of the Navajo folk-lore and dances and the varied arts of New Mexico and Arizona, having been discovered a little too late by people reared in a newer tradition, is often obscure to those who are born to it, and the counties to which native Irish is confined are Galway, Donegal, Kerry, West Cork and a handful of isolated places in Waterford. In Mayo and Clare and other places, where less than a hundred years ago it was the vernacular, it is remembered today only by a few aged people whose grand-children and great-grandchildren, instructed in the schools by teachers who them-selves have learned it from learners and generally hail from cities like Dublin and Cork, can scarcely understand them. A melancholy situation, whose brighter side lies in the characteristic contrariness of the fact that among city people of culture and imagination the language revival, as it is called, makes serious advances every year. A new literature is developing in which poets and writers of prose, themselves often native speakers from the remote places, are finding a new expansion and a great deal of en-couragement; the spelling has been logically simplified and standardized at last, the

28

Roman alphabet has finally replaced the picturesque but inadequate alphabet originally introduced by St Patrick (we say) and the future seems full of possibilities.

We can argue about the value or the worthlessness of this attempt to breathe new life into an ancient language on the borders of the valley of the shadow – and in Ireland we do – until voices grow hoarse and tempers frayed: we shall probably never agree. To be, as many Irish people affect to be, sincerely neutral about the subject seems to me out of the question. One cannot be neutral over a matter of life and death in one's own home, whether or not one cares for the person in danger, for however little one cares, one day, it is plain, there will be a corpse in the house, and until death comes the patient must be nursed and nourished or deliberately left to rot.

For myself, I confess it, I am wholly on the side of those who labour for the patient's recovery. That I am seldom in agreement with the manner of nursing or with the administration or the nature of nourishment, I also confess. Yet nurses and doctors alike, though I may curse them in my heart for what seems to me a mistaken, at times indeed a lunatic handling, are my sisters and brothers, for we have one love, one faith, one obsession, if you will. We can no more endure the image of Ireland without her own language than an Englishman, a Spaniard or a Frenchman could endure the image of their countries without English, Spanish or French. Literature and the drama have always been the chief medium Ireland chose for her expression, and it is one of our regrets that so much of these forms has been written, for over two hundred years, not in the country's own language at all, but in English. It is a regret, not because we believe Irish to be a better language than English. It is older, it is purer in origin, but it is not better. Indeed, because of a hundred obvious historical circumstances, chiefly of a depressing nature, English in many ways is more flexible, more developed, more equipped. But every country in the world has some innermost secret, and each secret – this to my mind is at the heart of our belief – has its own utterance, and the secret of Ireland can be communicated fully only through the language of Ireland. It can never find its fullest utterance in English poetry or prose, even when the writer is Yeats, whose inspiration and material were drawn almost entirely from Gaelic sources; even when the writer is Synge, whose actual medium of expression – that curious language he learned from the farmers and the tinkers of the countryside, and with which he enchanted so many millions of English and American ears – was simply a wellnigh literal translation from the older speech. Shakespeare himself, even when he wrote of Egypt or of Rome, revealed but a portion of their essence through his music, whose secret was not that of Egypt or of Rome at all, but of England, and that secret grew out of the woods and the rivers of Warwickshire and Essex and out of the houses of timber and brick built by Englishmen among their 'spreading oaks and pleasant meads', and that secret can be known and expressed only through the broad and sonorous music of the English tongue. The tender irony, the sensuous all-embracing secret of the châteaux and cities and vineyards of France can be apprehended only through the sensuous and tender irony of the French tongue itself: it is impossible to think of Racine, of Baudelaire, of de Musset, of Cocteau, of France herself, in any other way. The secret of Germany lies in the depths of pine-forests, of crooked medieval cities; in Spain a like mystery hides in the glare of sun and shadow, of bare brown hills and groves of cork and olive-trees, and only Spanish or German speech can give to these things their full celebration. In Ireland the mystery lives among twisted thorn and rowan trees, beside grey stones and churches and under ancient cairns and cromlechs: it is inherent in the scent of furze-blossom and turf smoke and it shines through the bleak purity of mountain lakes and twilit hills, and though the Irish way of writing or of speaking English hints unmistakably at these things, nothing but Irish itself can tell the whole of the tale.

Enemies of Irish, if the talk turns on the interest or the aesthetic importance of nationality being inseparable from its one unmistakable hallmark, which is language, often quote America. They always did: they always will. They forget that the language and individuality of America and of Ireland are two completely different questions. The history of North America, as far as Europeans were concerned, is that of a series of English, French, German, Dutch and Spanish explorers and colonists who discovered a new and marvellous continent and who created there a new and, in the main, marvellous civilization based upon old English, French, German, Dutch and Spanish traditions. It was natural and inevitable that the language spoken was to be English, French, German, Dutch or Spanish. What else could it have been?

Nationality, that can be as tiresome and inflammatory in the political sphere as it is various and fascinating in the sphere of the arts, is simply individualism *en masse*; its ultimate and uncontradictable signet and symbol is language. A nation that has lost its own language has lost a part of its identity, its individuality, and therefore of itself. It has become an incomplete and merely imitative entity.

A nation that never had its own language is certain to have made its national début as a colony springing from the roots of some older nation. As soon as its own nationality is established it begins, consciously or unconsciously, to develop a language of its own. That is what America is doing now.

The Irish question, however, is not one of colonization. The problem is not the same. On the one hand we have the story of a people developing an old tradition in a new country; on the other that of a people conquered by a neighbouring people and standing firmly against them by upholding whatever of their own tradition they may be able to preserve. The neighbours conquer the country; the people reject that conquest on the grounds that they are of a different origin and tradition from the conquerors and that, rightly or wrongly, they wish to remain themselves.

Yet in the present century, as in past centuries, some of them seem willing and ready to accept the language of the conqueror as their only medium of expression. Why?

Language is not merely the badge of a nation's individual existence: it is the very life-blood of its deepest thought, and one can no more think of Ireland as an entirely English-speaking nation than we can think of England as a nation speaking only Irish.

If history could have been reversed, if this had happened, we can guess at the result. Ireland would have been cited by the world – quite correctly – as the leader of English thought and intellect: as the true conquerors and possessors of English genius. Englishmen who wished to maintain a separate individuality in French or German or Spanish cities, or trains, or aeroplanes, would have been mistaken for Irishmen: and, very understandably, they would have resented it.

'We're not Irish: we're English', they would have protested in purest flowing Connemara accents, and their position – in the eyes of the world – would have been ludicrous. And irritatingly appealing.

So is ours: unless, somehow, we manage to preserve our language. Irish, Scots Gaelic, Breton and Welsh are the sole surviving examples of the Celtic speeches which once were spoken throughout western Europe. They are the only link that still exists between Greek and the spoken languages of the north: they are the bridge flung between Sanskrit and modern Italian and English itself. They, and the Scandinavian languages, are the only northern European answer to the mythology of Greece and Rome. They are the background of our true claim to national distinction: they are our only unquestionable claim to a sane reason for existence as separate nations: and if we, in Ireland, lose that claim, however divided in political or commercial fact our destiny may be, we may as well resign with a becoming frankness our right to be called anything but 'a province', our right to be styled, in truth, 'a nation once again'.

Ireland, if her own language dies, must in honesty accept a subsidiary relationship with England, from whose utterance her own will differ as vaguely in outline to the world that lies beyond the world of English literature and drama as the literature and drama of, say, Bavaria differs vaguely in outline from that of Prussia, or the Andalusian from that of Castile, or the Cornish or Northumbrian from that of the rest of England. And this acceptance may not be as crushing a defeat as stubborn and insatiable Gaelic minds imagine. For myself, the image of Ireland without Irish is insufferable, but if it is to be it would be well to accept it without the futile added quibble that, because of a different racial origin, of a few distinctive habits of expression, of a diverting dialectical form of English (which becomes daily more and more akin to the English of journalism, of radio, and of a quaint form of Americanese, less and less akin to the speech of Synge and O'Casey), the illusion can be kept up that England has not won the day in language and in literature, and that Irish literature in English, at its most assertive and distinctive, is anything more than the continuation of a contribution to the literature of England.

There could be worse fates than to add our share, as our writers have done in the past, and are continuing to do to this day, to the fire of a tradition that includes Chaucer and Shakespeare and Keats. Yet the feeling persists that another fire is smouldering still among half-forgotten ashes and must, by this means or that, be fed. After all there is only one sort of enemy that the Irish language has to fear. It is not the open opponent who comes to us with drums from Stormont, but the half-believer in our midst who throws up despairing hands at the language itself because of the stupidity of certain of its advocates. Such a man is the brother of the philistine who casts a suspicious eye upon the Muses because of the charlatans who kneel in mockery at their feet, of the doubter who denies the existence of God because he has stumbled over the body of some faulty monk asleep at his prayers.

Literature alone can re-open the eyes of the intellect: those eyes that have been closed by indifference, by hatred, or by that scorn which springs from a lack of understanding. The saints perished because their persecutors could not fathom their minds. Keats died through the blindness of his critics. So it is with the Irish language which stands in graver danger at the hands of the Irish people themselves – O'Connell was one of many tragic examples of men who, 'like the base Indian, threw a pearl away richer than all his tribe' – than it ever did at the hands of English despots bent on a brilliant unified design for living of which Irishmen of distinction happened to disapprove.

Unlike many Southerners, who for the most part have never crossed that tragic farce we call The Border and therefore should express no opinion at all (yet who in the land of Patrick, Brighíd and Colmcille can hope for that sort of a miracle?), I have a *grá* for the North of Ireland. (*Grá* is the Irish for love and is pronounced, according to English phonetics, as *graw*.) I say the North of Ireland from a force of habit acquired during the early twenties of this century, because the term since then has been a political, not a geographical one, and applies only to a portion of the North. For although the counties of Donegal, Monaghan and Cavan belong, by all the laws of geography and nature and tradition, to the northern province of Ulster, the majority of their people proved some years ago that they preferred Irish rule to English, and so they are no longer considered as belonging to what, colloquially, we mean when we speak of the North. That expression is intended to bring to the mind those six counties where the majority, having fought like mad for numberless years against what was then known as Home Rule, were themselves the first to achieve it.

That is only one among many facts that help to make the ideals and principles of the six counties appear to the rest of us a little eccentric; that helps, too, to foster the bitterness between ourselves and them. But sometimes we have been a little eccentric too, and in many ways we are unfair to them. Just as the Germans think that the French are all tricky and frivolous, and the French think that the English are all prudes and hypocrites, and the English think that all other nations, while being possibly amusing, are certainly unfortunate in not being English, so the majority of the people of what is called Southern Ireland are convinced that the people of the six counties are all harsh, pragmatical, cold, bigoted and rude. All the Protestants, that is; for the Catholics of the North, who in the main are the true natives of Ulster and are of equally Irish stock as any Kerryman or Galwegian, they have nothing but sympathy, and here their judgment is nearer the truth. For the problem presented in Ulster is one of plantation, and north-east Ulster is by no means the first plantation that Ireland has known.

Since the time of Queen Elizabeth the First, the English had continually experimented with plantations all over Southern, Eastern and Western Ireland (this fact accounting, of course, for the variety of English surnames throughout the country), for it was hoped, presumably, that by mingling Irish blood with English the people would grow gradually more amenable to English rule. The plan never worked very well because the English planters (apart from a few influential families who maintained a frosty distance, married each others' cousins, and held themselves aloof), the simple and impressionable creatures, got on, for the most part, extremely well with the Natives, frequently adopted their religion, frequently married them, and became, as the saying went, more Irish than the Irish themselves. Well, the latest plantation – it happened during the last years of the 17th century – was that of the north-eastern counties of Ulster, of all Ireland the most stubborn and ferocious in their resistance to English ideas, and it was cleverly decided to carry out this latest planting of the North, not with Englishmen at all, but with Scots. Chalk cliffs, apple orchards and Anglicanism gave place to granite rock, oat-cakes and the Presbyterian Church. Celt in fact met Celt, and the result was and remains a stubborn and at times sinister history of battle with a lot of funny local stories from both sides in its wake (these in Ireland are the inevitable accompaniment to any event of national or personal significance) and a trail of endless mutual animosity that stretches from London – which helps to finance it all from the Northern side – to the rest of the world that, understandably, remains indifferent to the whole question.

Belfast is the capital of the Six Counties and its people are not by any means invariably harsh, pragmatical, cold, bigoted or rude; nor are the majority of the people of Derry, Tyrone, Armagh or any of the other Northern counties I know. Some of them, of course, have all these distressing qualities, but the same thing could be said of many people in other places. Even in Italy, even in Greece, even in Southern Ireland, one meets them here and there.

It must be admitted, however, that few districts in the civilized world have any annual festival to compare with Ulster's Twelfth of July, when the most beautiful lilies, of a colour that matches the name of the ancestral home of King William of Orange, are plucked from Protestant gardens to be worn on Protestant breasts where the beating of the heart rises to the same pitch of ecstasy (though not of volume) as the beating of a thousand drums, beaten and beaten from early morning until late into the night with bare fists and palms as well as with sticks until the blood flows down over the parchment and Ulster manhood is appeased. Sashes and banners of the same fiery orange hue are everywhere in this all-male rhapsody of fever and fervour, sashes and medals and badges worn by boys of eight and men of eighty: bowler hats, black suits, stiff collars and dark ties are *de rigueur*; the streets are impassable and uncrossable, sometimes for hours together, and the poor Papists remain – if they are wise – indoors and wait, presumably, for the dawn of the Thirteenth to break, when things simmeringly settle down again.

It is an astonishing sight, the Twelfth of July, whether one witnesses it in some little country town, or on the historical streets of Derry, or parading on Donegall Square about the City Hall of Belfast, a vast and sumptuous monument of mingled tastes

34

that echo all known and unknown styles from the Albert Memorial to the City of Dreadful Night: so astonishing, indeed, in its rigid militant bleakness, its harsh asser-tiveness of Sunday best and orgy of primary colours punctuated with white and black, that the cultured citizens of the Six Counties should go down on their knees (what-ever their political passions may be) and pray for an Ulster Douanier Rousseau to paint it before its drumming, cymbal-crashing splendour fades away. How long, oh Lord, how long?

There are poets and painters who live in this oddly ugly city that has for me a peculiar charm of its own. Perhaps it is the charm of disguise, for that is one of the first things you notice about it: it wears a mask. Everything possible is done to hide up the fact that you are in Ireland at all: the Irish language is seldom heard and never seen: the buses and telephone booths and pillar-boxes of the Six Counties, and of Belfast in particular, are of the same uncompromising scarlet as those in England: the Union Jack flies and God Save the Queen is sounded with far more frequency. *Ulster Is British!* is the motto everywhere, and but for the blue mountains at the end of the streets, the quality of the light, the sigh of the wind, certain faces and voices, certain hints of melancholy and of magic lightly touching you as day passes into night, you might easily believe yourself to be in Bradford or Manchester. Put a foot out of the towns that may be big or small and you have no doubts at all as to where on the map you are walking or driving: for as Katherine Tynan wisely remarked in some half-forgotten children's book of many years ago, 'the Glens of Antrim are as Irish as Limerick or Clare'. They are as lovely too: Antrim and Down have a beauty as intoxicating as that of Sligo or of Kerry itself. The northern coast, encrusted with its Giant's Causeway, its Dunluce Castle, its bays and promontories and wild stretches of green and grey and gold cliffs that tumble down to the sea, beyond which, far away to the north-east, you may watch the hills of Scotland gathering the faint clouds about their heads, is unsurpassed. And this remains true today in spite of The Border, whose most tragic drawback to my mind is that it has momentarily separated, within the con-fines of one small nation, in the arts, in the world of politics and science and com-merce, all Irish energies and their communication. The thought and sympathy and action of what should be a united people have been split into two unequal parts, Dublin and Belfast alone finding themselves, in spite of the negligible distance be-tween them, almost as intellectually divorced as, say, London and Moscow.

How long, oh Lord, how long?

Rightly or wrongly Ireland remained neutral in the Hitler war, and during it, and during the couple of tonic years of austerity that followed, it was easier even than usual to recognize English visitors, because already from a distance you could perceive, if you had sufficient sensibility, the aura of a keenly anticipatory appetite, and as you drew nearer you heard the word 'Steak!' with more frequency than was usual. 'Steak!' they murmured, or 'Steak and chips!' according to their individual social conscious-ness, and their numbers grew so rapidly that while many Irish hands were rubbed with delight at this renaissance of *tourisme*, many Irish heads, unaffected by dreams of profit, as they were not placed on the shoulders of farmers, cattle-dealers, butchers or restaurateurs, began to wag and many tongues to prophesy of a new English invasion. Because, you see, the searchers of steaks often took a liking to the country and even to its people; the climate, after all, was not much heavier to bear than their own, and the income-tax a good deal lighter. So they took to renting or building houses in every conceivable locality; a few wealthy Americans – unaffected by thoughts of nourish-ment even in the 1940s – followed their example, and the numbers of non-Irish resi-dents in the Republic today is considerable. The Americans and the Germans for a period took over many famous beauty-spots like Killarney and Glengariff, and hotels and lake-side restaurants of an elegance hitherto rare became a commonplace. On the whole I think everyone is pleased about this. For one reason (human), of course, the influx has brought a good deal of prosperity to rural places that for years had known little but their own loveliness and what seemed an unalterable poverty; for another reason (gastronomic), it was found pleasant for those among us who hanker, however unworthily, for the pleasures of the table when the day's work or the day's idleness is over in a town of which one has had more than enough by the time the sun has begun to set; when one begins to long for mountain air and mountain peace, yet dreads the grey potato, the bog-sodden cabbage, the grease-riddled rasher, the unrelenting mutton chop. Besides, it is amusing for Irish people to meet from time to time people who are not Irish, who will not inevitably lead you to some too, too solid groundwork of some

VI THE RED DRAWING ROOM, BANTRY HOUSE, CO. CORK

The marble mantlepiece is French 18th-century work. It is surmounted by an Aubusson tapestry, one of four panels decorating this room said to have been made for Marie-Antoinette on her marriage to the Dauphin. (*See also* plates 53–55.)

too, too familiar speculation about... the language or the Pope or the penal days or the future or the fiendish behaviour of the opposition or the true facts about your Aunt Kate or the standoffishness of the Protestants or the hopeless taste of the Catholics... *My Darling that new drawing room of theirs oh haven't you seen it an orgy of off-white and squalor me dear or – what That One said about her own harmless poor little devil of a husband if you please* [A One, in Ireland, is invariably female] *footless with drink she was as usual of course or – what that Other One saw with her own two eyes going on in Nora's car in the very shadow of the Pro Cathedral – wait till I tell you you'll die when you hear... curdle your blood or – how young Murphy... no not at all no Seán's the brother not Declan... well since Declan had had just the one unspeakable little verse play... too dank for description darling... put on in that cellar in Cork... complete and abject failure even there of course... Dotey sure Declan couldn't write his name let alone a play but I needn't tell you he thought he was God Almighty and not only come to live in Dublin but had planked himself for life on the two poor Pats in their studio no less – and what about Con Cooney's new book NOT being banned after all and him banking on that for the English sales God – and did you hear about the heir to Ballyslattery me Dear ah no not at all no you have it wrong no you were listening to gossip – you know I often wonder is there any reason at all why the individual soul should exist at all upon my soul I often wonder is the whole damn thing some sort of a vast atavistic illusion out of some sort of a vast lost jungle what is the soul at all unless it's the personality well what happens will you tell me that when the worms get going on your eyes and your tongue – now listen to me you you know what I'm going to tell you you're drunk sure of course you are sure my God listen to you look at you but...*

VII LANDSCAPE NEAR KILLORGLIN, CO. KERRY

The bog is here seen in its summer guise, bright with cotton grass. In the background are Macgillycuddy's Reeks, so called because they are thought to resemble turf stacks (*see* plate 25).

VIII COTTAGE NEAR CLIFDEN, CONNEMARA, CO. GALWAY

It is common in Ireland to find a cottage built alongside a ruin. Tenants formerly built and repaired their own houses, usually without assistance from the landlord, and there was little encouragement to repair a house that was held on only a short lease. Thus when a house fell into complete disrepair, it was easier to build a new one than to put the old in order. The thatch on this cottage roof, held down along the eaves and at the ridge with ropes pegged into the thatch at intervals, is typical of the district. (*See also* plate 79.)

wait now wait did you know that Desmond and that English One were not only married they're also going to have A Baby God wouldn't it freeze the marrow in your bones...

Such *causeries intimes* are general throughout the country in large or small places and between all persons regardless of age, rank or sex: such trifling facts merely determine the timbre of the voice, the pronunciation of the words, the use of slang which, by the way, changes in Ireland far less rapidly than in America or England. A One, as I have said, is and has been as far as living memory can stretch, a female, and one about whom the speaker feels condescending if not scornful; Your Old One is your mother; a Bowsie is a definite but endurable ne'er-do-well; a Gowger a disagreeable one; a Get an unspeakable one; Dote or Dotey is a Darling; a Guerrier a rowdy inclined to the favourite weakness of Don Juan; Janey Mac a censored form of Jesus Jack (although, inexplicably, it becomes in Cork Janey Martin); a Notorious Old Bottle or a Tramcar is a prostitute; a Mott a dubious though possibly attractive woman; The Brother may be the brother of the speaker or that of his hearer; Your Man is any male person who happens, at the moment, to be under discussion, and so on. And none of these terms is in favour among the refined, who prefer the more varying fashions of American and English fancy, but they are understood (though frequently disagreed about) by everyone in the land.

So naturally we like, if only now and then, to meet with strangers whose outlook and utterance are so different from our own and who – can it be believed? – find us as odd and amusing as we themselves. The Irish mind has an unexpected and not infrequent likeness to the old-fashioned Continental conception of the old-fashioned English mind, being easily shocked (though by different things), profoundly reserved (though on different matters), unalterably activated by humbug (though in a different way), incurably self-conscious (though from a different angle), and incurably conservative (though about different subjects). It is also bewildered but as a rule (unlike the English) fascinated by foreigners, it is astonished when it discovers the English are human (as well it may be), it cherishes a naïve and terrified admiration for the Germans, is shocked and thrilled to the marrow by the Americans, feels a deep kinship with the French, whom it deeply mistrusts, and has no attitude at all towards the Japanese who, it seems, are here in their hundreds but are seldom, if ever, visible and who, if they were, would merely remind it of Madame Butterfly if only from sheer force of contrast in appearance.

I have spoken of Ireland's real secret being for the most part discoverable by chance in certain moods of her countryside, in lonely reed-grown pools and half-forgotten places among rocks and heather and bogland, in ancient steep-roofed churches that still stand, though now they are broken and ivy-covered, among deep woods or in the shadow of bare mountains. There are the skeletons of cottages and cabins too; empty and roofless they are now, their hearth-stones and doorways choked with nettles and dock-leaves, and there are many older and more significant monuments of pagan and Christian days. They have changed their names, some of these haunted places: Brugh na Bóinne, The Faery Fortress of the Boyne, is now known as New Grange to English speakers having no knowledge of the Irish tongue; Dubhad, close to New Grange – both of them are in the rich pastureland of County Meath – is called in English Dowth. But most people know that Brugh na Bóinne, that hollow hill into whose depths the pilgrim enters, when he has been presented with a lighted candle (difficult to manipulate for he must crawl through a narrow passage on hands and knees), was the temple of Aonghus, the God of Love, the Gaelic Eros, described in the Bardic tales as a naked youth bearing a harp in his hands and about his head an ever-fluttering circle of white birds; or that Dubhad na Ríogh was the burial place of Kings and Druids. (I have not been in Brugh na Bóinne for some time, but hear a rumour that the pilgrims' approach is now lit by electricity.)

Both of these centres are set about with great grey stones engraved with the spiral symbols of eternity used by the Tuatha Dé Dánaan, the red-headed interpreters of the elemental powers, of the recurring patterns of reincarnation, of the influence of the sun and stars and moon over the nature and the destinies of mankind.

'And ancient Ireland knew it all', Yeats wrote towards the last days of his life. And at New Grange, on the grassy mound that forms the roof of the temple, there are thorn trees, sacred to the Gods and all the multitudinous peoples of the Sidhe: the white limestone quartz believed to have covered long ago the whole surface of the hill are only visible now in glimmering patches here and there. But within, all is preserved except, it may be, for the colour, antiquarians and visionaries alike believing that these places once may have glowed like the peacock's tail: now they are as grey as time.

There are many such mounds and stones, hillocks and holy wells in Ireland, and certain great forts like that of Staigue Fort in Kerry, and others in Clare and Galway and Sligo; all these things point to a forgotten past, and it may be to a forgotten wisdom, and one can arrive at most of them within a couple of hours or so from the centre of Dublin. Even the most monstrous and magnificent of all, Dún Aonghusa, that faces the Atlantic from the cliffs of Inis Mór, the biggest of the three islands of Aran, is within four or five hours from the capital. Or it would be, were it not for the capricious humour of the tides, for when you have arrived at Galway you may have to wait for hours for the Aran steamer with its cargo of human beings and, often, of indignant cattle and pigs that are hauled on board by ropes and alternately encouraged and bullied into their place with yells and endearments and the inevitable accompaniment of belabouring sticks and answering bellowings.

The invisible multitudes of whom I have spoken are numerous still in the haunted places where once they were worshipped and still, deprived of their ancient power and bent on preserving it, they often steal human beings. They leave an *iarlais*, a changeling, in their place: a sickly, wizened and sometimes spiteful creature who bears a warped resemblance to the beloved stolen one, but who in fact is but a mockery. The Faeries are especially covetous of newly married brides and of male children under the age of puberty. In Aran, in remote parts of Connemara and in other wild places, you still see little boys running on the roads and over the fields in the summer-time dressed in long trailing skirts of woven scarlet or magenta wool that belong to their mothers or sisters, bunching them up in their hands that their bare feet may carry them the faster. They are disguised as girls, for whom the Good People or the Gentry – propitiatory terms of politeness, for the unearthly creatures are easily offended – have less use than for boys, and it is devoutly hoped that the invisible Kidnappers, for all their mercurial subtlety, are simple enough to be deceived by these evasive tricks. Nor should you ever praise the beauty of a baby in its cradle or its mother's arms without piously adding 'God bless it!', for the Good People have eyes like hawks, and are always watching and listening; they have a boundless desire for what is admired. They are beautiful themselves, you see, they are powerful and faulty and full of joy, of weakness and of violent prejudice, and they live far beyond our conceptions of right and wrong; and in this, as in many other things, they resemble the Gods of Greece.

There are Christian monuments and memories everywhere as well: indeed, the early Christian period stretching from the 4th to the 9th century bears witness to the richest of all Ireland's contribution to the arts. At Cashel, where castle and fortress and chapel rise out of the hill like a broken crown of pearl and tarnished silver set on a fantastic head of green and grey; at Clonmacnois, at Armagh, at Glendalough, at Mellifont and the fabulous Ballintober – Baile an Tobair, the Town of the Well – where a solitary priest is gathering help towards the Abbey's restoration. In all these places there are altars of stone and crucifixes enwrought with the woven serpentine motifs of Celtic ornament, sepulchres and round towers and sarcophagi and small stiff figures of stony saints and monks, and of priests and kings and poets bearing croziers or sceptres or harps in their hands and showing the heavily pleated cloaks, the naked feet, the faces that seem to express nothing but a ghostly astonishment under the long elaborately combed and dressed hair and beards of immemorial Irish fashion. And there are many jewels as well, golden chalices and torcs and bracelets of bronze and silver, though these for the most part are stored away in museums or in the libraries of universities, like the illuminated pages of the great books of Kells and Durrow where the monks' hands have left page after page of decoration intricate as a spider's web, and in colours that glow so richly one seems to be looking into caskets filled with crushed jewels.

Ireland, you see, is full of the strangest contradictions and in this indeed she is not unique, though it would seem that nowhere else, in Europe, at any rate, are there such extremes of desolation and brilliance, poverty and riches, apathy and energy, idiocy and intellect, blindness and vision, wanton callousness and imaginative sympathy, mental fog and cerebral clarity. The weather repeats the fickle uncertainty of these humours: there is no answer can be found to the stranger's question, 'What is the best time of the year to visit your country?'

There is no best time on which to lay a finger: you may breakfast in your garden on sudden golden mornings of February or November, or huddle over the fire on some icy summer's day when the calendar informs you that this is indubitably the month that some Irish-American writer, whose years in New York or California had filled his head with memories of gold, once called 'the miracle of an Irish June'.

A miracle indeed, when June decides to behave like June, but one never can tell. The clouds are always ready to be swept like an old shawl about the head of Cathleen, the daughter of Houlihaun (Caitlín ní Uallacháin), but the sun, almost as frequently, is ready to shine out too at the most unlikely moments, and with her (the sun, in the Irish language, is a feminine noun, and was to the ancients a mother), after an hour or so of shrouded tears, come the rainbows, two or three of them together, it may be.

The landscape itself, as I have suggested, continues this capricious behaviour. You may pass from the desolate places beyond the Gap of Dunloe in Kerry, magnificent in their nakedness as the Burren in Clare or the savage fastnesses of Donegal, where man may ask for bread but will certainly be given a stone, and within an hour or so you will be among the flowering groves and dells of Killarney among thorn trees and coppices of briar coloured like the rose as they lean among wild rhododendrons over pools of lapis-lazuli where herons, standing on one leg, gaze at their own shadows in the jewelled water. And you will see ravines and wooded cliffs that seem carved out of precious stones green and black and russet moss starred with tiny flowers, wild roses, dragon-flies, golden faery rings in the grass, deep woods honeycombed with sunshine, and, encircling them all, the mountains of the Kingdom of Kerry dyed with blue and darker blue and silver and rose as they rise from the wild earth to the sky.

It is an obvious reflection that all movements and moods in the arts are coloured by reaction against the movements and the moods that immediately preceded them, and I have often felt that the prevailing spirits that guided taste at the turn of the century, in the English-speaking world particularly, sprang from the fate of one individual writer. When we talk of the 1890s and their attitude towards art and life, we usually have in mind the first five years of the decade, whose outstanding manifestation was known as the Decadence, a movement which collapsed with the trial and imprison-ment of Oscar Wilde, and the immediate reaction – it is really very striking if you study it carefully – took four forms of expression: the sudden rise of 'healthy philis-tinism' whose prophet was Kipling, the asexual astringency of George Bernard Shaw, the return of the innocent fantasies of childhood led by Kenneth Grahame and J. M. Barrie, and the renaissance of various forms of mysticism, whose expression ranged from the writings of Yeats and AE to those of Francis Thompson and Lionel Johnson, from Druidism to the Catholic Church. In the case of Yeats this re-awaken-ing of a preoccupation with things of the soul led, unexpectedly enough, to the crea-tion of the first theatre Ireland had known that was to be something more than a call-ing-place for touring companies from England: it was to be a creative home for the Irish theatre, and its plays, the poet hoped, were to be in the main 'remote, spiritual and ideal'. A forlorn hope at the best, for when has the art of the theatre been con-fined within the boundaries of the infinite? Always, at its best and at its worst, drama has been concerned with conflict, with imperfection; with Oedipus tortured by con-science or with Scapin caught in the net of his own intrigues, with Othello made grotesque by jealousy or with Charley's Aunt tripped up by those trailing skirts; sel-dom is it absorbed by the spectacle of the Holy Family seated in eternal bliss among clouds of glory. Such conceptions of the finality of perfection are for poetry and paint-ing, not for the stage, whose art is not only essentially popular but also essentially communicative, vivid and various in mood and expression. And so it was that the Irish theatre Yeats had planned with such elaborate hopes was turned, to his most understandable dismay, into a happy hunting-ground for the Irish realists of the photo-

44

graphic school and for the makers of comedy, both high and low, and was destined at last to produce the present-day Irish stage formula for that curious mingling of racy, well-worn quips and drab or prosperous domestic cheeriness that entitles a play to be known as representative Irish drama. John Millington Synge was the first and the last writer who combined the poetic temper of Yeats's ambition with that grim and earthy sense of mingled passion and farce that outraged the fools and turned the heads of the wiser men, and forced the English-speaking world to look at the Ireland he showed them, an Ireland that Lover and Lever and Boucicault had seen only through the eyes of caricature. In Synge there was little of the caricaturist or of the photographer, still less of a reporter of those literal platitudes so often accepted as realism. In spite of his accounts of listening through chinks in the wall (or was it the floor?) of some remote hostelry to the rich conversation in progress in the kitchen – one does not doubt this: one has few doubts about the essential teller of truth that lived in Synge – we can trace in every line of his plays the creative ear and hand at work on the English spoken in Wicklow or West Kerry or the County Mayo as clearly as we can trace in Shakespeare that ear and hand at work on the speech of his own War-wickshire, accepting and rejecting, transforming and colouring, dissecting and reveal-ing what was originally but raw material, a mere audible fact. Synge, in short, was a born dramatist, and his plays, as well as creating a storm of protest, filled the theatre for the first time in its early years and paved the way for the later and, as I think, lesser figure of O'Casey and for the declining school that followed him.

For all that, the Irish theatre had been created by Yeats. It was through him, essen-tially a poet, a philosopher, a man driven by mystical curiosity rather than by dramatic instinct, that it came into being, and his achievement was more a national than a per-sonal triumph. Its early period is best described, it may be, by his own account of the result of his labours with Lady Gregory and others in a report written in the year 1901, in which he speaks of 'an excellent little company which plays both in Gaelic and English... I may say', he continued, 'that we have turned a great deal of Irish imagina-tion towards the stage.'

The work of the Abbey Theatre was, and is, fundamentally to reveal Ireland to her-self and then to the world. That is why it is hard to join the hue and cry against its present-day writers, for all self-revelation begins, even if it does not end, by a peering at one's own face in the glass, and the Abbey, with all its glaring faults, reveals more or less accurately what the glass gives back. If its present offerings show a decline in imagery, in richness, in dramatic depth of colour and form, it may be because Ireland herself, in her transformation from the royal, restive, war-bedraggled captive that she was into the youthful, muddle-headed, ambitious débutante she has become, is at a stage of her history whose result may be more stimulating in the promise of future development but is at present less dramatically interesting.

As a very young man, after ten years in London, seven of which were spent as a boy actor in the theatre, I returned to Ireland, my head filled with the thoughts of Ireland's need for a theatre in the capital city that could show something more than the Abbey, where only a portion of Irish life was interpreted. What other stage had Dublin? A couple of good theatres for touring companies that contributed nothing not shared by Belfast, Sheffield, or any fair-sized provincial town: a handful of well-intentioned in-experienced groups playing, now a translation from the Russian or the French in cur-tains, now a London success of seven seasons ago in borrowed stock scenery, and one or two amateur musical and operatic societies. Ten years later I met, in Anew Mc-Master's Shakespearean company, that for some years had brought classical tragedy and comedy to the Irish country towns, Hilton Edwards, an English actor who had served his seven-year apprenticeship in Shakespeare, five of them at the Old Vic, where he played both in Shakespeare and in opera; and finding that our ideas about the theatre, starting from different angles, matched almost perfectly once a certain meeting place was reached, we created, with the help of others, the Dublin Gate Theatre, whose aim was to present an international repertoire of foreign masterpieces (we made no allusion to lesser plays), that Dublin was unlikely to see unless we brought them there, and to experiment in methods of production unhampered by the demands of the commercial theatre. We also hoped that the foreign masterpieces, both old and new, would guide the younger Irish writers to fresh forms in the expression of certain sides of Irish life the Abbey had never explored, and in this we were not altogether dis-appointed. Expressionism was the fashion of the day and it was this manner that coloured much of our early work at the Gate. Denis Johnston was our most important discovery as a dramatist, and in him, as I have written in a book called *Theatre in Ire-land*, my partner Hilton Edwards 'found the modern writer who exactly suited his own talents as a director... Both of them had been influenced by writers like Joyce, Toller and Kaiser, or by directors such as Reinhardt, Meyerhold and Piscator'; and I have

IX KILLARY HARBOUR, LEENANE, CO. GALWAY

We are looking in the opposite direction from that shown on plate 80. The fjord is running inland, overshadowed by the Maamturk Mountains.

46

written in the same book 'it is with a certain tranquil, autumnal sort of enjoyment that one reflects how they in their turn begat in Dublin a small but clamorous brood of followers who, as Yeats would have said, wore their "embroidered coats" and who, before you could say Finnegans Wake, popped up in every nook and cranny to provide the public with so many black drapes, shafts of light, crooked architecture, obscurely bawdy jokes, menacing hands, oddly shaped rostrums with steps, choral interludes, and gentlemen rushing from their seats in the stalls to join the frolic; so many plays about the Spirit of Ireland not being all one had thought before or even during the year 1922, so many demonstrations to prove that the Celtic Twilight was the phoniest fiction ever thought up on the Euston Road, and that the Real Ireland, and especially the Real Dublin, was much closer to the older quarters of Berlin or Chicago than to the Land of the Young, that the parentage, and indeed the grand-parentage of these activities was, most understandably, forgotten.

'In their turn the younger groups were all disdained by their enemies – who for the most part did and do very little at all that might commit them – as "Twentyish". The truth of the accusation does not rob it of its inherent shallowness. For almost everything in the theatre today that does not hark back to some yet older fashion betrays, remotely or clearly, the influence of the twenties...

'Our beginnings in 1928, like the beginnings, almost thirty years previously, of Yeats's National Theatre Society that was later to become the Abbey, were at once wildly ambitious and severely, almost ostentatiously small.'

The obstacles facing us were at times spectacular. The summer of that same year had seen our opening of Taibhdhearc na Gaillimhe, the Gaelic Theatre of Galway, with a production of my play *Diarmuid agus Gráinne*: it was a year of many events for us. Hilton Edwards and I produced in Dublin – he directing, I designing, both of us acting all the time, and occasionally designing and directing plays in Irish in Dublin

X THE HIGH CROSS, DEVENISH ISLE, LOUGH ERNE, CO. FERMANAGH

The High Cross in the foreground stands in the centre of the upper cemetery of the island, to the south of St Mary's Church (*see also* plate 113). It appears to date from the 15th century from the evidence of the ogee arch and the Tudor leaf design at the top of the shaft, which exactly resembles the decoration of the ogee arch of the door leading into the sacristy from the church. This opening bears the inscribed date 1449. The niche in the face of the shaft shown in the photograph is a very odd feature, for it is too small to have held a statue. The head of the Cross may possibly not have formed part of it originally.

and in Galway – some three hundred plays by authors from nearly every country in the world. Shakespeare, Yeats, Ibsen, Aeschylus, Shaw, Tolstoy, Sheridan, Kaiser, Čapek, Wilde, Martínez-Sierra, Dostoyevsky, Cocteau, O'Neill, Strindberg, Chekhov, France, Wilder, Coward, Lenormand, Achard, Longford, Hsiung, Williams, Quintero and Gertrude Stein have been among our authors; and here and there a new Irish play has appeared which hints at the discovery of the qualities we seek: a vision of certain phases of national life other than that of cottage or tenement; 'a style that is at once analytic and formal; an attempt to express the heart beating under the ribs as well as the colour and texture of the covering flesh. The actors of our Gate Theatre, having more ground to cover than their brothers at the Abbey, have a correspondingly wider technical range and, I think, a less sharply defined manner. But as the Abbey failed, by the very strength of its popular appeal, to realize the dream of its creator for a poet's theatre where the players, robed dimly and chanting in many voices, should re-create the arts of minstrelsy, of dancing, and of a symbolic celebration of the mysteries, so have we failed in the main to discover among our authors the man who shall write for us our masterpiece.'

And since our earliest days other groups have appeared and disappeared: Lord Longford's company that, until his death in 1961, shared the Gate Theatre with us, he playing there for one half of the year and we for the other half, and the Globe and the Pike and the Players' Theatre and the Lyric Theatre Company and the Orion Players and the Gemini Players and a dozen more.

The Abbey is subsidized in what, nowadays, is a small way: still, it is regularly subsidized, and survives: other companies, as I have hinted, have vanished or have made, and are making, new appearances, many of which suggest some likely ultimate disappearance; with the present exception of Orion and Gemini and of our Gate Productions that still make sporadic manifestations of an obstinately lively activity. But for Yeats, none of us would have existed at all, and how long any of us will continue to exist side by side with television and all the rest of it, God only knows.

It was believed during Yeats's lifetime, and the belief still flourishes (is kept alive indeed, not by the general public, Irish or otherwise, who have no particular interest in such things, but by the poet's most ardent and self-declared admirers, critics and analysts), that the Celtic Twilight, originally the title of his earliest prose work, was merely a convenient label, lent by the book and its mood, for a certain phase in the treatment of Irish subjects that became fashionable for a while during the 1890s and the turn of the century. In a certain measure this was true: the title perfectly fits the earlier poetry and prose of Yeats himself, and of his contemporary, the visionary poet and painter, AE. It is also descriptive of the style and subject-matter of the many disciples these two men had bewitched to make them follow their lead. It left its mark, too, on a whole generation of Irish and Scottish writers, and of readers of English everywhere. It was a fashion that reflected as much as it helped to create the prevailing temper of its period: it walked at times hand in hand with the Symbolists and certain of the Impressionists of France and the pre-Raphaelites of England; its utterance harmonized with that of the later Wagner and with almost all of Debussy and its manner suited perfectly its subject-matter. At its worst its form may be detected in the graphic arts among the imitators of Burne-Jones and in many French theatre posters riddled with tall, yearning ladies doing nothing in particular among thickets of attenuated water-lilies and tubercular-looking daffodils, and in literature in certain slim grey volumes of poems like those of Max Beerbohm's Enoch Soames; at its best it is found in *Tristan und Isolde*, in *L'Après-midi d'un Faune*, in the clouds and flowers and shadows of Monet, and in the earlier writings of Yeats and the discovery of the dying world of Gaelic legend and myth whose echoes, still miraculously alive, he and his contemporaries in Ireland heard from the lips of the country people sitting by turf-fires.

It is always amusing to look back at a mode of expression that has passed into history, but in the pursuit of this idle pleasure, as far as the Yeatsian Twilight is concerned, I have always felt that an important fact has been overlooked. Yeats, in giving a title to his accounts of dreams and visions among the peasantry of Sligo and Galway, did not simply invent a literary label: he made a discovery. Because of his passion for supernormal mysteries, he stumbled into a region of twilight that was and had always been a fundamental truth not merely concerned with climate, though that was a part of its essence, still less with a manner that happened to be for the moment in fashion.

A few years earlier Vincent van Gogh had groped his way out of Holland to the revelation of the supreme moment of Provence in the round glare of the midday sun. To Yeats in much the same manner the supreme moment of Ireland was revealed at the hour of twilight, and its mood, that hovers between day and night, between light and dark, between waking and sleeping, between, in so many familiar cases, sobriety and intoxication, is at the heart of Ireland's being.

No person and no thing can quite escape it. Even the United States of America, that is so much nearer to our island than to Great Britain – I am not thinking only of geography – although it swiftly gives to our emigrants and their descendants many practical lessons of great, and less great, value about daily life, cannot altogether blow away the mists that descend upon the Irish mind when the day's work is done. The door of the office is closed, the car is driven into the garage, the files are replaced on their shelves, the long-awaited guests have arrived and been given their welcoming drink, or have departed after the last *deoch an dorais*, the drink of the door, or the one for the road, or what you will, and lo! the magic is resumed; the leaves whirl round, whether the winds that blow them come from Brugh na Bóinne or from Calvary, and the Irishman, whether he has failed or succeeded in life, is on his knees or staring out of the window as night falls. And if the eyes of the body can see nothing but the towers and spires of New York or Chicago, or the London or Liverpool roof-tops, the eyes of the spirit are looking on remembered mountains and lakes and rivers and towers, such as those you will find in this book, and these images will awaken dreams of fathomless wonder beneath and beyond themselves and of which they seem indeed but the earthly mask. The reaction against the out-dated label of Celtic (or any other racial) Twilight, and of its consciously wistful or mysterious approach has only added to the complexity of the reality itself. As the brightest light will throw the deepest shadows, so the Ireland of today, with its new-found eagerness to be, as you might say, in the swim, its passion for the progress of factories and sky-scrapers, and destruction and replacement and speed, its odd indifference to its own rare and ancient treasures, does but deepen the incongruity of the immemorial setting of these things, as the lately rushed-up monuments of glass and steel in modern Cairo but deepen the deathly silence of desert and gilded tomb. The admirable, if self-conscious, reaction against the school of the Celtic Twilight among writers from Shaw to Joyce and Johnston and Beckett and Behan and O'Connor and a dozen more, merely accentuates the national inability completely to escape, not from its old-fashioned manner but from its under-lying truth.

The only way out, indeed, seems to be a literal one: a definite and final turning of the back on the country itself with all its snares and enchantments, a definite and final turning of the face to England or some other less dream-infested clime. Sheridan, Goldsmith and Wilde were, for a time, highly successful in this, though they too had their moments of being once more enmeshed: in Wilde's case especially this was so; magic and mystery were as deeply woven into his being as were wit and the fore-shadowing of disaster. As for Shaw, that brightest beacon among the leaders of the Anti-Twilight crusaders, he was in fact the most vulnerable of them all: a happy, busy, practical man who at any moment would himself be 'caught in the cold snows of a dream'. His mouthpiece, Mr Larry Doyle, of the architect's London firm of Broadbent and Doyle, suddenly remembers the colours in the sky at home, the 'lure in the distance, the sadness in the evening' and away he goes on his 'torturing, heart-scalding, never satisfying dreaming'. At any pause for breath in the overwhelming traffic that whirls through the head of James Joyce we are listening to Dublin women whispering together as they wash their clothes and drink their bottles of stout while day draws into night, or to the voice of Anna Livia Plurabelle herself as she rolls from the mountains to the sea. More than all of them, Beckett is an eternal prisoner among haunted shadows: Paris herself can do nothing to deaden his ears to their whispering and murmurings. And so it is with the other arts: painting and sculpture, after long fallow years in a country where ears have been for centuries more sensitive than eyes, are both showing signs of a vigorous awakening life; music, too, is at the beginning, as I believe, of a creative period. In all these things the shadow in Ireland will mingle with the light, the dream with the reality, the sun with the rain, the breaking of morning with the dawn of darkness.

For Ireland, the home of incongruities and contradictions, something of whose face you see in this book, hovers in truth between all known facts and unknown mysteries; an island that is the last outpost of Europe and lies alone in the waters, as I have suggested, with no country on her right hand but her ancient neighbour, her conqueror, her enemy and her probable future ally, and on her left hand nothing at all but the wild ocean, with America far away on the other side of the world. In olden times she was named, as she still sometimes is named, Inis Fáil, the Island of Destiny, and what is past or present or to come, as she herself knows well, lies on the lap of that inscrutable Goddess.

MICHEÁL MAC LIAMMÓIR

An extract from Micheál Mac Liammóir's *Theatre in Ireland* is used by kind permission of the Cultural Relations Committee of Ireland, Department of External Affairs.

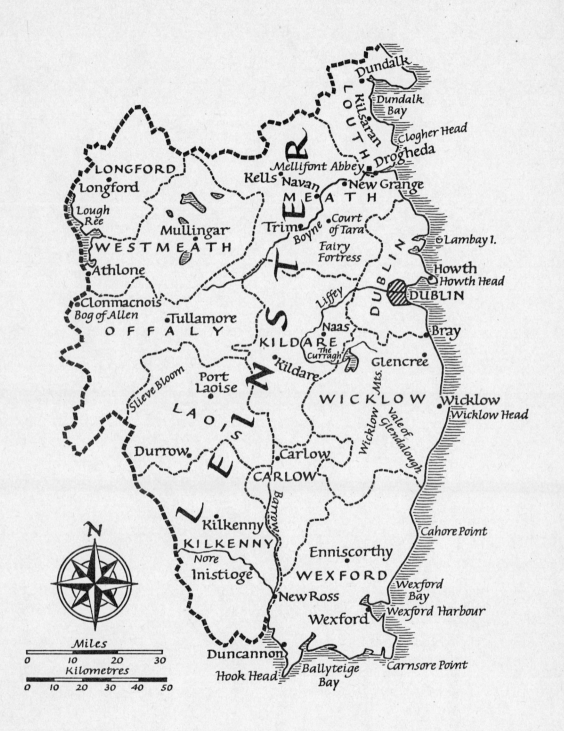

2

3

7

10

9

20

29

32

38

39

NOTES ON THE PLATES 1–40

1 THE LIFFEY FROM THE METAL BRIDGE, DUBLIN

We are looking downstream in the light of a spring morning. The dark, yet translucent water recalls the peaty source of the river in a bog of the Wicklow Hills. To the left are Bachelor's Walk and Eden Quay divided by the O'Connell Bridge. This was built as Carlisle Bridge in 1791 to the design of James Gandon (*see* notes 5 and 10) as a link between Sackville Street (now O'Connell Street) and the newly fashionable north-eastern quarter of the city. The bridge was rebuilt in 1880 to accommodate the full width of Sackville Street, and though the Portland stone balustrades of the original structure were preserved, Edward Smyth's fine sculptured keystones were removed. It was the intention of the Corporation to re-name the bridge when it was altered, but influential residents objected and made application to the courts, with the result that on 19th June 1885 Vice-Chancellor Chatterton granted a perpetual injunction against the Corporation to prevent any change of name. Though now invariably called after Daniel O'Connell, the bridge is still registered as Carlisle Bridge. (*See also* plate 41.)

2 PLASTERWORK FROM ST VINCENT'S HOSPITAL, 56 ST STEPHEN'S GREEN, DUBLIN

No. 56, together with Nos. 54 and 55, has been a hospital since 1834. It is thought that the house was designed by the brothers Robert and John West, for the owner, Lord St George, had already made their acquaintance through a business transaction when he decided to build a house in St Stephen's Green in 1760. Robert West was both a master builder and plasterer, and it is to him that the brilliant rococo stucco work scattered in pale colours over the walls and ceiling is attributed although, as so often, different hands may have collaborated in the execution of the work.

Many a plain, flat Dublin façade conceals exuberant delights in this medium which, closely associated with Catholicism in the countries of its origin, Italy, Austria and Germany, seems peculiarly suited to the climate of Ireland. Mr C.P. Curran (in 'Dublin Plasterwork', *Journal of the Royal Society of Antiquities of Ireland*, 1940) shows that a body of skilled plasterers were pursuing their craft in Dublin from the late Middle Ages and that the magnificent flowering of the art during the 18th century was inspired by the French style of the Regency and Louis XV, which itself derived from Italian sources. The liberating influence was that of two brothers, Paul and Philip Francini, who came of a Florentine family domiciled in France from the end of the 16th century. The Francini arrived in Ireland in 1739 to work on the ceiling of the saloon at Carton House, Co. Wicklow. Before their advent, Irish plaster ceilings had been divided into compartments of heavy static ornament in the Palladian manner. At Carton a bolder, looser sense of design is combined with broadly modelled figures of gods seated and reclining on clouds, busts of classical poets and tossing *putti*. The Irish plasterers were quick to seize on the possibilities of the new unconfined style and created a vividly spontaneous, dramatic and wildly asymmetrical art of stucco.

The windblown niche enclosing the figure of autumn, from the ceiling of 56 St Stephen's Green, is a typical example of the Dublin style of the mid-18th century. This detail does not, however, show another speciality of Irish ceilings of this period, although it figures conspicuously in the design as a whole – the partiality for birds. Birds in flight, birds perching and nesting, birds are everywhere clamorous in Dublin rooms, and Robert West was the outstanding master of the bird motif.

After about 1770 the delight in natural forms and vigorous modelling gave way to the flatter, colder, more restrained style associated with the name of Robert Adam (*see* plates 73, 103 and 107).

3 Doorway of No. 41 Merrion Square, Dublin

Doorways are among the minor but intense pleasures of Georgian Dublin. The characteristic design of these round-headed doorways with their enormous segmental fan-lights is based on a motif which was invented by Palladio and which first appears in the gallery arcades of the Basilica at Vicenza. The arches there have side openings introduced, not only to lighten the arcade but to reduce the uncomfortable width of the openings decided by those of an earlier building behind them. The Dublin architect needed a generous arch to articulate and enrich his extremely austere and rectilinear façade, and also, to light the entrance hall. The device of the side openings enabled him to achieve his ends and to gain additional light without having recourse to a door of disproportionate width. In English doorways of the period door and fanlight are usually set within a pilastered, pedimented or hooded frame of wood or stone and the fanlight is consequently of only the same width as the door. No. 41 Merrion Square was built in the last quarter of the 18th century and the detail shows Adam's influence. A feature commonly found in Dublin doorways is the lantern fitted into the fanlight.

4 MERRION SQUARE, DUBLIN

The second largest of Dublin's great squares was laid out in 1762 by John Ensor who, with his brother George (*see* note 106), had come to Dublin from Coventry some time in the 1730s. Many of the windows on all sides of the square have lost their glazing bars and balconies, and thus the delicate balance of the transition from brick to glass has been seriously disturbed. Nevertheless the impressive austerity, harmony and reticence of the Irish Georgian style and the poetic light that softens the cliffs of brick are magnificently displayed in this noble vista.

The line of Merrion Square is continued by Upper Mount Street to Mount Street Crescent and St Stephen's neo-Grecian Protestant Church. It was designed by John Bowden and completed by Joseph Welland in 1824. The portico is based on the Erechtheum and the tower on the Tower of the Winds and the Monument of Lysicrates. Among the great names in Irish literature and poetry associated with Merrion Square are those of Sir William and Lady Wilde, who lived at No. 1; Daniel O'Connell, whose home was No. 58; Sheridan Le Fanu, who owned No. 70; and W.B. Yeats, whose Dublin residence was No. 82.

5 THE FOUR COURTS FROM MERCHANTS' QUAY, DUBLIN

Just as Gandon's Custom House presides over the eastern reaches of the Liffey, so his Four Courts dominates the western stretch. The arresting feature of this composition is the huge mass of the pilastered drum and cupola, set back behind the pediment and towering above the screened courtyards on both sides of the central block. Viewed from the opposite quay or from Father Matthew Bridge, the masterly design triumphs yet over the mechanical, lifeless aspect imparted to the stonework during restoration, after extensive damage had been inflicted on the building during the fighting of 1922. Cement was used instead of stone to replace the entablature and the stepped blocking course of the dome.

The Four Courts, originally the seat of the four courts of the judicature, Chancery, King's Bench, Exchequer and Common Pleas, and now of the Supreme Court as well, is essentially the work of James Gandon, though he adapted his design to an unfinished building on the site by Thomas Cooley intended as a Public Records Office. Cooley had planned a single quadrangle, entered through an open screen on the south side. He died in 1784 when only the south and west sides had been completed. In the following year it was decided to transfer the Four Courts from St Michael's Hill to Inns Quay, and Gandon was asked to incorporate Cooley's work in the new building. The present Four Courts was begun in 1786 and completed in 1802.

Gandon reduced the size of Cooley's quadrangle, substituted his monumental domed block for Cooley's east range and replaced Cooley's screen by one of greater magnificence, pierced by a grand triumphal arch. This new quadrangle with its screen was repeated to the east of the dome. The sculptor of the five figures crowning the main pediment, *Moses* flanked by *Justice* and *Mercy* with *Wisdom* and *Authority* seated on the corners, was Edward Smyth (1749–1812). Smyth also carved the splendid trophies of arms over the triumphal arches. The crowning feature of these before restoration was a diadem instead of a sphere.

6 DOORWAY, HENRIETTA STREET, DUBLIN

Henrietta Street, now sombre and derelict, apart from its lively inhabitants, belongs to the first of two great building periods in Dublin. The houses went up a little before 1730 and set a model of princely magnificence to the city. They were built by Richard Cassels or Castle (*see* note 15 and plate 72). This doorway is an earlier, undeveloped version of the kind shown in plate 3, which became the accepted Dublin type. The side lights have not yet made their appearance and the square pilasters with their brackets look as though they were meant to support a pediment or hood in the English manner. Instead they are surmounted by the semicircle of the fanlight, the leaded panes of which have long since vanished.

7 BOOKSTALL OFF BACHELOR'S QUAY, DUBLIN

Bookstalls are less readily associated with the Liffey than with the Seine, perhaps because Irish literature had almost ceased to exist before the Revival in the 19th century, perhaps because censorship discourages a taste for reading. The greater number of the books on this stall are dusty relics of the early part of the century, chiefly of patriotic interest, with a sprinkling of novels by such writers as Charles Lever, Gerald Griffin

92

and Charles Kickham. The browsers are sheltered from a cold east wind by the bulk of the Dublin Woollen Co. building. It is a Sunday morning, litter blows about the stall and the chill air echoes with the peal of bells in minor keys.

8 THE IRISH HOUSE, O'MEARA'S, DUBLIN

The imagery decorating this folly public house on the corner of Wood Quay, close to Fishamble Street where Henry Grattan was born in 1746, symbolizes some of the crucial events in Irish history. The six towerlets surmounting the building take the shape of the tapering round towers of pre-Norman Irish monastic settlements. These were used not only as belfries, but as watch towers and places of refuge. They thus recall the greatness of Early Christian Ireland and also stand as a protest against agression. The chief of the naturalistically-coloured stucco reliefs adorning the Irish House shows Henry Grattan making his last speech in 1800 to the Irish Parliament, the independence of which he had been largely instrumental in creating in 1782 and which now, by the Bill uniting Ireland and Great Britain, was abolished. Grattan's impassioned lament for the Constitution was a superb example of the Irish talent for sustained eloquence and verbal felicity: 'Yet I do not give up my country', he ended, 'I see her in a swoon but she is not dead; though in her tomb she lies helpless and motionless, still on her lips is the spirit of life and on her cheeks the glow of beauty.'

The occasion of this speech is further illustrated by the relief shown in the photograph of Erin weeping on a stringless harp, while the figure of Daniel O'Connell beside her symbolizes the later emergence of Ireland as a nation.

9 THE NELSON PILLAR, O'CONNELL STREET, DUBLIN

On 8th March 1966, some months after this photograph was taken, the Nelson Pillar, once known as 'Dublin's Glory', was destroyed. Designed in 1808 by William Wilkins and erected by a committee of Dublin bankers and merchants, the great column recalled the air of dignity and vitality which must have informed this commercial thoroughfare when it was first laid out in the 18th century by the banker, Luke Gardiner, as a tree-planted residential street with a fashionable promenade down the middle. The statue of Nelson was carved by Thomas Kirk (1777–1845). The cage round the base of the figure is a recent addition, to prevent suicides.

10 THE CUSTOM HOUSE, DUBLIN

The Custom House, one of the only two works of architecture on a grand scale on the banks of the Liffey, is best seen, like the Four Courts, from the opposite quay because, again like the Four Courts (plate 5), it is largely a mechanically executed restoration after destruction between 1916 and 1922. In 1921 the great building was raided by the Dublin Brigade of the IRA and blazed for five days. The original Custom House was designed by James Gandon (*see* note 5), who had been brought over to Ireland from London for the purpose by John Beresford, Chief Commissioner of the Irish Revenue.

The main features of Gandon's design, a long façade with projecting Doric portico, central block and end pavilions dominated by a drum and melon dome, are still clear, but the present contrast between the extreme horizontality of the main structure and the aspiring dome is now too emphatic. The transition was formerly more subtly organized by means of the high roof and the chimney stacks of the central block, and a sense of hovering movement was encouraged by four allegorical statues crowning the pediment. The sculptures which survived the fire, largely the work of the talented Edward Smyth, are of exquisite quality. The relief group in the tympanum of the pediment is an allegory of the *Union of Britain and Ireland*, two figures seated on a shell drawn by sea horses, with Neptune driving away Famine and Despair. The noble keystones symbolize the Atlantic Ocean and the thirteen principal rivers of Ireland. The arms of the Kingdom of Ireland, with the device of the Harp of O'Carolan surmounting each of the end pavilions, are perhaps the finest of all the carvings for vitality and crisp detail.

The statue of *Commerce* crowning the dome is also by Smyth. His work was brought to Gandon's notice by Henry Darley, the general contractor. Gandon was a pupil of Sir William Chambers and imbued with the principles of Palladianism. Whereas Chambers, for all the perfection of his work at Trinity College (plate 11) and at the Marino Casino on the outskirts of Dublin, saw in Palladio's art no more than the cold application of the Vitruvian rules, the façade of the Custom House, strongly and rhythmically animated by the groups of columns, all of the same great height, and the dome soaring up from the loosely encircling peristyle of the drum, show a perception of the true originality and excitement of Palladio's work – his interest in chiaroscuro and movement.

11 THE EXAMINATION HALL, TRINITY COLLEGE, DUBLIN, SEEN FROM THE ENTRANCE TO THE CHAPEL

Trinity College was founded in 1591 by Elizabeth I at the instance of the Protestant

94

Archbishop Ussher, after attempts to revive a much earlier foundation had been made in vain in 1547, 1565 and 1584. Pope Clement V had granted a Bull as far back as 1312 for the establishment of an Irish university, and rules for the government of the masters and scholars of such a university were drawn up in 1320. But in 1363 a petition to Pope Urban V alleged that there was no Irish *studium*. Succeeding years record the endowment of a lectureship in theology by the Duke of Clarence in 1384 and the provision of stipends for university lecturers for seven years in 1496. Civil disturbances continually hampered the development and expansion of the university, but it existed until the Dissolution.

The present College stands on the site of the Augustinian Priory of All Hallows, founded by Dermot III of Leinster. The buildings were ready for the admission of the first students by 1593. Among the many distinguished men who followed them to Trinity were Congreve and Farquhar, Swift, Oliver Goldsmith, Burke, Oscar Wilde and Synge.

Nothing survives of the College earlier than about 1700, for the buildings were reconstructed on a grand scale in the 18th century. The photograph shows the vast cobbled West Court (also called Parliament Square because the Dublin Parliament defrayed the building costs) and a pedimented building, which is the exact counterpart of that in which the camera is set up. They each terminate a wing of the front range and were designed by Sir William Chambers and carried out by Graham Myers between 1781 and 1790. They are unmistakably Palladian with their rusticated lower storeys, pedimented porticoes and balustraded parapets, and they might appear a trifle heavy were it not for the perfection of the proportions and the delicacy of the capitals, curved with curling fern fronds, flowers and pomegranates. The spiralling wrought-iron lamp brackets were designed by the architect. The interiors of both buildings are enlivened with plasterwork by Michael Stapleton (*see also* plates 107 and 108).

12 St George's Church, Dublin

This noble church in the classical manner is the work of Francis Johnston, the first Irishman to become widely celebrated as an architect. Though there were other talented Irishmen building during the 18th century, such as Robert and John West (*see* note 2) and John Roberts (*see* note 46), they were overshadowed by alien architects. The district in which the church stands has declined, and many of the original Georgian houses in its vicinity have been replaced by modern working-class flats, but the shape of the site, devised by Johnston as a setting for St George's, remains. The church is fronted by a sweeping crescent at the junction of Temple and Hardwicke Streets and the ground falls away in steps behind the building, thus placing the utmost emphasis on the extremely tall spire. The upper stages of this spire are reminiscent of those of James Gibbs's St Martin's-in-the-Fields in London, but the lower stages of Johnston's tower reverse the proportions of those in Gibbs's spire and are far less bulky, thus achieving a soaring movement which counteracts the pronounced horizontality of the façade with its severe Ionic portico. Whereas Gibbs's tower sits back incongruously on the roof of what is visually a classical temple, Johnston has pushed the tower of St George's so far forward that it is possible to see the designedly narrow though monumental portico as the base from which the spire springs. Under the portico are three superb carvings by Edward Smyth, keystone heads of *Faith, Hope* and *Charity*.

The church was begun in 1802. In the year of its completion, 1814, Johnston presented a peal of bells to St George's. He was interested in change-ringing and had a miniature church tower with bells erected in his garden at No. 64 Eccles Street near by. Johnston is buried in the cemetery of St George's in Whitworth Road, but his gravestone can only be found with difficulty, so worn is the inscription. He died in 1829.

13 THE INTERIOR OF THE CHAPEL ROYAL, DUBLIN CASTLE

A comparison of this photograph with that on the opposite page shows that Johnston was as much at home in the Gothic as in the classical mode. The interior of the Chapel Royal, completed in 1807, is one of his most brilliant designs and among the most enchanting works of the whole Gothic Revival. It is often compared for accuracy of detail with the church which is generally cited as the first instance of correct neo-Gothic, James Savage's St Luke's, Chelsea, London; though they are alike in the sharp precision which characterizes every detail of both interiors, there is no other point of similarity. The Chapel Royal, white and gold, starry-vaulted, is an exuberant and personal rendering of the combined Early English and Perpendicular styles. The period might still be that of 18th-century Arbury and Tetbury in England, for the dazzling effect is achieved by a re-interpretation of the visual aspects rather than of the structural principles of medieval architecture. The soaring fan vaults, the urbane decorative heads and the crisp capital foliage of the Chapel Royal are not of stone: they are masterpieces of the plasterer's art, the work of John Smyth (son of Edward) and of George Stapleton (son of Michael).

14 THE MONKEY PUZZLE AVENUE, POWERSCOURT, CO. WICKLOW

The magnificent demesne of Powerscourt on the lower slopes of the Wicklow Mountains was laid out during the last century by the Sixth and Seventh Lords Powerscourt, descendants of Sir Richard Wingfield who acquired the property in the reign of James I. It was probably the last great landscape garden to have been created. By the time it was completed in the 1870s the horticulturist was already ousting the artist in the sphere of garden design. The Irish climate encourages luxuriant growth and Powerscourt is splendidly timbered. The avenue of exquisitely symmetrical, dome-shaped Monkey Puzzles, *Araucaria umbricata*, with their glossy foliage and thick glaucous trunks, is but one instance of the astonishing fertility of Ireland. Rare Dragon trees, so tender that they can survive only the gentlest air; the Blue Gum, aromatic cousin of the magnolia; the *Drimys winteri* and the tall Sitka spruce can all be seen in their pride at Powerscourt.

15 THE PEBBLE-PAVED PERRON, THE TRITON POOL AND THE DISTANT SUGAR LOAF MOUNTAIN, POWERSCOURT, CO. WICKLOW

The austere mansion of Powerscourt was built in 1743 of silvery granite by the German-born architect Richard Cassels on an eminence overlooking a prospect which offered the finest possible setting for a great landscape garden. The ground fell away naturally to the south in a series of terraces to a sheet of water known then by the unaffected name of Juggy's Pond, while on the far side of a distant wooded valley rose the Wicklow Mountains culminating in the shapely cone of the Sugar Loaf, a smooth form of dove- or indigo-colour changing to the clearest pink in the light of the setting sun. Yet despite these obvious natural advantages a century passed before this romantic panorama was subjected to the controlling influence of art. The first stone of the terraces was laid in 1843. According to Christopher Hussey, the designer was 'a brilliant but dissolute character named Daniel Robertson', who suffered severely from gout in the humid climate and had to be transported about the demesne in a wheelbarrow clutching a giant bottle of sherry.

The Fifth Lord Powerscourt died in 1844 and the garden work came to a halt. It was not actively resumed until 1858 when the Sixth Lord came of age. The terraces were rapidly completed and Juggy's Pond became the great stretch of ornamental water now known as the Triton's Pool. From the first vast terrace, 800 feet long, below the house, a broad shallow flight of steps leads down to a wide lawn, and beyond this *tapis vert* is the remarkable perron with its cobbled ramps, the focus of the whole garden composition, going down to five further terraces and the Pool. The striking black-and-white patterns of the paving are composed of pebbles from the beach at Bray, and the geometric configurations were devised for the Seventh Lord Powerscourt by Francis Cranmer, antiquary to the Royal Academy and amateur astronomer. The bronze groups of *amorini* on the perron date from the 18th century and are the work of Joseph Marin. They came from Richard Wallace's French villa *Bagatelle*.

16 ROOF SLAB OF THE NORTH SIDE CHAMBER, NEW GRANGE, CO. MEATH

New Grange, Dowth and Knowth are the most important and conspicuous burial mounds in a prehistoric cemetery on a tongue of land, about five miles from Drogheda, lapped by the River Boyne. The most prominent of the three, New Grange, is indeed one of the most impressive megalithic monuments in Western Europe. In ancient Irish literature the cemetery is sometimes referred to as Brugh na Bóinne, 'Palace of the Boyne', thus emphasizing its royal character, and it is traditionally associated with a mysterious personage variously named 'Oengus an Brogha' (Oengus of the Palace), or 'Oengus mac in Dagda' (Oengus son of the good god). The burial place may have been connected with royal Tara only twelve miles away. Modern scholars (cf. *New Grange* by Sean P. O'Riordan and Glyn Daniel, 1964), basing their conclusions on the comparative study of similar tombs in Portugal, Spain and north-western Europe, incline to the belief that the mounds are the tombs of important chiefs of prospecting and trading communities, who first came to Ireland from Iberia at the end of the 4th millennium BC. New Grange is a Passage Grave, a variant of the basic plan of a tomb chamber approached by a passage, and it is suggested that while the first Irish Passage Graves were built between 3500 and 3000 BC, New Grange may be roughly dated *c.* 2500 BC. It is the work of people who knew the use of metal and who had knowledge of the smelting and casting of copper tools. Externally it is a huge irregular mound about 42 feet high, though it must originally have been more, tree-grown now and surrounded by a kerb and a stone circle. The entire surface of the mound was probably once covered with a layer of fragments of quartz so that, as at Ballymacgibbon (*see* plate 81), the glittering hemisphere of the tomb would be conspicuous from afar. New Grange is cruciform in plan, a straight entrance passage, 62 feet long, leading to a roughly circular burial chamber with an end and two side recesses.

A number of the massive stones of New Grange are decorated with carved spirals, lozenges, triangles, zigzags, cup marks, concentric half-ellipses and composite patterns, all of which are found in the repertory of megalithic art elsewhere. The most elaborately carved stone of all is the roofing slab of the north side recess, shown here. The decoration was almost certainly done before the huge stone was placed in position. These devices are far more significant than mere ornament and, as they are examined, resolve themselves into formidable, mysterious figurative compositions involving the schematized eyes, breasts and face of the great Earth Mother goddess. Many archaeologists have commented on the astonishing resemblance of the spirals of New Grange to those of Mycenean art and have inferred a direct influence, but recent scholarship, as we have seen, ascribes a much earlier date to New Grange and regards the Boyne tombs as a reflection not of Mycenean civilization but of the pre-Mycenean civilization which flourished in the Cyclades, Troy, Crete, Malta and Iberia in the 3rd millennium BC. The continuing tradition evolving from this schematized art can be traced in the decoration of the monuments of not only prehistoric but also Christian Ireland, in the ornament of the Iron Age stone at Castlestrange (plate 82), for example, and in many of the motifs on the sculptured crosses and portals and in the illuminated manuscripts of the Early Christian period. The roots of Celtic art are to be sought in the compelling carvings of New Grange.

17 VIEW FROM THE CENTRAL CHAMBER INTO THE NORTH RECESS, NEW GRANGE, Co. MEATH

The photograph shows the wonderfully impressive structure of the tomb at New Grange, which combines the megalithic and dry-stone walling techniques. The walls are constructed of huge upright stones called orthostats. One of the interesting features of New Grange is that, whereas in many known works of megalithic architecture the stones are only roughly dressed, they have here very often been carefully smoothed and shaped. The recesses are roofed with great horizontal megaliths, while the principal chamber has a magnificent corbelled vault (successive layers of overlapping stones), the best-preserved in any chamber tomb in Europe. The vault springs from dry-stone walling retained by the orthostats. The latter stop a good deal short of the vault, which starts from behind the lining slabs. The roof of the Early Christian Gallarus Oratory (plate 62) is constructed in exactly the same way.

On the floor of the north recess, visible in the photograph, stand two large flat stones, one above the other, hollowed out into the form of shallow basins. Perhaps the cremated remains of the deceased were deposited with grave goods in these basins. Similar basins stand in the other two recesses. Smaller basin stones (known as bullauns), associated with ritual sites, both ancient and modern, are objects of special veneration in Ireland. Any water which accumulates in them is said to possess special virtues, akin to those attributed to holy wells (*see* note 37).

18 THE CROSS OF MUIREDACH, MONASTERBOICE, CO. LOUTH

Approached by a deep lane and encircled by an ancient wall, the monastery of Monasterboice is like a little city of the dead, where the ruins of two small churches, a tall broken Round Tower and three sculptured crosses rise from a forest of tombstones. Even in decay, Monasterboice vividly conveys the aspect of the native monastic communities of Ireland before the Continental monastic orders were established in the country. Instead of one central architectural complex there were a number of detached buildings, residential cells, study rooms, refectory and, scattered over the enclosure, a multiplicity of tiny churches or chantry chapels. The domestic buildings were often constructed of wood, but the churches and the belfry tower, which was also a watch tower and a refuge (*see* note 28), were built of stone from a very early date.

'Monasterboice' is a corruption of the Latin *Monasterium Boeccii* (the monastery of Boecius), the Latin form of the name of the Irish saint *Buíthe*, who was born during the latter half of the 5th century and probably died in 521. One of the twenty-two recorded abbots of Monasterboice was Muiredach, son of Donnall, who died in 922; it is believed that he is the man whose name is inscribed on the smaller of the great standing crosses of Monasterboice, for the monument belongs exactly to his period. Apart from the names of the abbots between AD 759 and 1122, little is known of the history of the monastery. The Cistercian Abbey of Mellifont was founded close by in 1142 and completely overshadowed the small native foundation. The last recorded abbot of Monasterboice, Fergna mac Echtigeirn, died in 1124.

The massive Cross of Muiredach is the finest of the three crosses on the site and perhaps the most splendid of all Irish sculptured crosses. Such tall stone standing crosses are found only in Ireland and Great Britain. The practice of erecting them appears to have originated in Northumberland early in the 8th century and to have been introduced into Ireland about a hundred years later. It is thought that these crosses replaced earlier monuments of wood. They served as boundary marks or preaching stations, or they were expressions of the piety of some donor. The churches of the Irish monastic communities were too small to hold large congregations and pilgrims would gather round the cross, the preacher taking his text from the scenes sculptured upon it. The crosses all conform to a basic pattern. They are set on a rectangular base or pedestal in the shape of a truncated pyramid, from which rises a four-sided shaft with a cross bar and with a wheel (a cosmic symbol) surrounding the intersection. The top of the cross, as here, sometimes takes the shape of an oratory with a gabled and shingled roof. The surface of the cross is usually divided into panels containing abstract ornament or figure subjects.

The photograph shows the east face of Muiredach's Cross. At the top, below the sloping roof of the miniature oratory is depicted a subject often represented on these crosses: *The Visit of St Anthony to St Paul in the Desert* and the breaking of the loaf mysteriously brought down by a bird for their sustenance. This subject is rarely treated in Western Europe but it occurs also on the 8th-century Ruthwell Cross in Dumfriesshire. The head of Muiredach's Cross is entirely filled with a dramatic rendering of *The Last Judgment*. The beardless, draped figure of Christ dominates the scene, holding in one hand the Cross and in the other a flowering sceptre. At his feet St Michael weighs the souls of the dead. The Devil, lying beneath the balance, tries to drag down the empty scale as the Archangel thrusts at him with his staff. The left arm of the Cross is filled with the choir of the Blessed; in the right arm the doomed are harried by the Devil, wielding a three-pronged fork.

The scene immediately beneath *The Last Judgment* shows the Adoration of the Magi. On the panel below this is depicted Moses striking the Rock. As the water gushes forth two rows of Israelites line up with bowls to take a draught. The two principal figures in the next spirited relief are David, holding in one hand his shepherd's crook and in the other his sling, and Goliath, who has fallen to his knees, clasping sword and round shield in one hand while he presses the other to his head. The remaining two figures are Saul, seated, and Jonathan, each armed with sword and shield. The heads of Adam and Eve, under the Tree, and of Cain and Abel can just be glimpsed at the top of the bottom panel. The scenes are informed with great intensity, concentrated as they are in strictly confined areas. Although the figures have been skilfully adapted to fit the varying shapes of the panels and although, with their abnormally large, rounded heads, they make an almost abstract pattern, the sculptor has introduced a surprising diversity of animated gesture into each group. As an art form the sculptured relief derives from the Roman practice of decorating triumphal arches and columns with chronicles in stone and, although the Romans never set foot in Ireland, the Early Christian sculptured crosses are among the very few instances of an Irish art indirectly influenced by Roman example.

19 ST COLUMBA'S 'HOUSE', KELLS, CO. MEATH

This tiny church, for such it is, was completed in 814, some seven years after Abbot Cellach of Iona had transferred the league of Columban monasteries to Kells to escape from the menace of Viking attack. The church is among the principal remains of the Columban monastery and replaced an earlier building, destroyed in 807, which may have been of wood. It consists of a single cell measuring, inside, about 19 by 15½ feet. The walls show a considerable batter and are more than 3½ feet thick. The roof structure resembles that of St Kevin's Church at Glendalough (*see* plate 22), but this building is much more impressive than the little Glendalough church. To appreciate its truly monumental aspect, it should be seen from the other side where, with its steep roof and irregular but beautifully constructed and richly textured walls, it nobly confronts and dwarfs a featureless modern villa. The method of building differs from the dry-stone technique of the Gallarus Oratory (plate 62), in that the use of mortar has enabled the architect to construct a straight-sided corbelled roof, triangular within as well as without. Straight-sided roofs had a tendency to sag and the Irish mason countered this by building what may be termed a propping vault. The critical level in a straight-sided roof is about half-way up and it was here that the propping barrel vault was placed both in St Columba's 'House' and in St Kevin's Church. The upper part of the roof contains a croft divided into three parts by cross walls, each with a central opening. These walls help to support the corbelling.

The entrance in the south wall replaces the original west doorway which has been filled with rough masonry. Above it is a very small window with a triangular head, reminiscent of Saxon work.

20 MOYDRUM CASTLE, CO. MEATH

Hundreds of ruins bear witness to the turbulent history of Ireland and intensify the wild, melancholy beauty of the landscape. Many have been completely abandoned and are rapidly sinking into a state of utter dissolution. Such is Moydrum Castle. Destroyed in the 'Troubles', it was formerly the residence of Lord Castlemaine and was clearly a Gothic Revival building of great charm, probably of about 1830. Its language is essentially classical and horizontal with a strong Gothic accent. Before its rhythm was so rudely broken, the symmetry of the façade was absolute. The remains of a massive interior with classical columns, now thickly cloaked in ivy, further emphasizes the underlying horizontality of the design.

On the other side of the wall, bright with gorse, far down in a great boulder-strewn, heather-blotched waste, lies the valley of Glencree. The river flowing through it eventually becomes the Dargle and enters the Powerscourt demesne (plate 15) as one of the most awe-inspiring waterfalls in Europe. The bare uplands glimpsed behind the wall were once covered by a primeval forest of oak. The destruction of the trees began towards the end of the 13th century, when Queen Eleanor established timber works in the valley to provide wood for the building of her castle at Haverford. The wall or 'ditch', as it is called in Ireland, where the word is used in its older sense of 'dyke', a raised bank, is of a type common throughout the farming country of central Ireland. It consists of an earthen bank faced on one side (that shown in the photograph) with stones, and planted with brambles and gorse (whins) among the stones.

22 THE CHURCHYARD AND ST KEVIN'S 'KITCHEN', GLENDALOUGH, CO. WICKLOW

Glendalough ('the valley of the two lakes') lies in a steep, wooded glen watered by an enchanting stream and two lakes. It was by the upper of these lakes, a smooth, dark mirror for the frowning heights of Lugduff and Camaderry, that St Kevin settled as a hermit during the 6th century and was joined by a community living according to a common rule. The foundation grew and spread eastwards towards the mouth of the valley where the Glendasan River runs between mossy banks through a wide meadow. By the 12th century, Glendalough had become a veritable monastic city, a great centre of learning and pilgrimage. The ruins are extensive and deeply impressive. They include the remains of seven churches, a priest's house, ancient wells, a Round Tower, crosses and inscribed grave slabs. The whole complex of buildings is entered by the old gatehouse of the monastic 'city', two round-headed arches of granite blocks once surmounted by an upper storey. The church seen in the photograph, to which the absurd name of St Kevin's 'Kitchen' has only recently been given, is remarkable for its excellent state of preservation. It is constructed of local mica-schist and granite and consists of a barrel-vaulted nave covered by a steep, corbelled roof, with a small stone-roofed sacristy attached. Above the vault, in the roof space, there is a croft, as at Kells (plate 19). From the west gable rises a small belfry in the form of a miniature Round Tower. This belfry probably dates from the 11th century, but the main structure goes back to the same period as St Columba's 'House', though it may belong to a later decade of the 9th century. A chancel, still standing in 772 but afterwards destroyed, was added to the nave possibly at the same time as the belfry. The walls slope inwards in the traditional Irish fashion. The nave was originally lit by two small unglazed openings, one in the east wall, the position of which can still be made out, and one in the south wall. The former was blocked up when the chancel was added.

The ruins of the monastic city now stand in a cemetery, the tombstones of which date back to the early 17th century. No one can fail to be struck by the picturesque aspect of these stones, all of the same granite and shale as the remains of St Kevin's foundation, blotched with silvery lichen, lurching this way and that, deep in ferns, exotic mosses and brilliant, clutching ivy. Some of the most interesting carved stones, bearing 18th-century dates, are signed 'Denis Cullen'. They show the crucified Christ beardless as in the Early Christian manner, and the disciples and Roman soldiers appear in 18th-century dress.

23 CROSS IN ST KEVIN'S 'KITCHEN', GLENDALOUGH, CO. WICKLOW

This granite cross, known as the Market Cross, formerly stood on the Laragh road and may have been one of the preaching stations (*see* note 18) for pilgrims coming to Glendalough. The cross is of a type that appeared in Ireland only in the 11th century and belongs either to that or the succeeding century. It differs from the early High Crosses, such as those of Monasterboice (plate 18) and Clonmacnois (plate 27), in that the figure sculpture is restricted to the Crucifixion and a prominently depicted ecclesiastic, and the cross-head is relatively small. The iconography shows Late Romanesque influence: Christ is represented with inclined head and is wearing a short kilt-like garment. This cross is closely allied to that at Dysert O Dea (plate 57).

24 WEST DOOR OF THE CATHEDRAL OF ST PETER AND ST PAUL, GLENDALOUGH, CO. WICKLOW

The Cathedral is the largest and most imposing of the ruins at Glendalough. The nave is pre-Romanesque, the chancel dates from the 12th century. The massive, lintelled west doorway is the most ancient part of the building and its Cyclopean masonry recalls the remains of Mycenean architecture, a comparison further prompted by the sloping sides of the opening, a structural device intended to reduce the span of the lintel.

The venerable character of the architecture at Glendalough is enhanced by the texture of the local stone, granite and mica-schist, which is of a slatey quality, scaling off with the passage of time and patterning the structure with abstract shapes and indentations. It also provides ample foothold for the luxuriant, pallid lichen of the district.

A turf fire burns in every Irish cottage and the sweet scent of such a fire lingering in the damp air is part of every traveller's experience of the Irish countryside. The bog itself, silent and empty except for the short cutting season, spreading all over the low-land heart of Ireland and extending far into the mountains, especially along the western seaboard, is the most persistent element in the landscape and the source of the most strange and haunting of those effects of light and colour for which Ireland is famous. Purple and burnt sienna and patterned by dark, parallel trenches in spring, waving with bog cotton in summer, changing to russet and fiery red in autumn, the bog is at its most mysterious at dawn or dusk, glinting in the long rays of the rising or setting sun with an unearthly silken sheen. Turf bogs do not only provide fuel; they are a record of the past, preserving intact the seeds, fruits and pollen of cycles of vegetation as well as bones and objects of stone, metal and wood going back to the ice age, which is represented by the remains of the arctic willow and the giant deer.

The season for turf-cutting is April and May, the driest months of the Irish year. At this time the markets are full of bright new tools, factory-made now, for the most part, instead of smith-forged, but still available in considerable variety. The common spade (differing, however, from the English type in its narrow blade and foot plates) is used to remove the top layer of fibrous peat to a depth of about a foot. The bog parings are spread between the cuttings, as in the foreground of the photograph, where they provide a dry footing for the man wheeling away the turves in his slatted wooden barrow. There are two methods of cutting, vertical or 'underfooting' and horizontal or 'breasting'. The former, which is being followed in this terrain near the saddle pass of Sally Gap between the Djouce and Gravale Mountains, is generally used on thin up-land bogs, while 'breasting' is reserved for deep lowland bogs. For both methods the tool used is a spade known as a 'slane', a narrow, straight-edged steel blade with a wing set at right angles to it. The wing is set forward at a rather sharp angle for 'under-footing' and backward for 'breasting'.

A foot-rest is provided on the side of the slane opposite the wing and slanes are made for both left- and right-footed workers. The purpose of the wing is to detach a turf at a single stroke of the blade. The proportions of blade and wing vary according to the size of turf required and also to the type of bog. It is essential that the slane should be as light as possible and the spade-tree is therefore usually made of elm or larch. The traditional tool was fitted with a cow's horn as a hand grip. The wet turves are spread on the ground for about a week, then put in little groups of about a dozen or so leaning together in the shape of a pitched roof to catch the wind. Then, throughout the summer months, the turves are turned and stacked into larger and larger piles, either alongside the bog road or against the house gable. The various-sized piles are known as turn-foots, castles, clamps, rickles and reeks. (*See also* plate 75.)

26 Tintern Minor Abbey, Co. Wexford

Situated near the head of Barrow Bay where wooded, pastoral country slopes down to sandy creeks, Tintern is one of the most romantic of the many ruined Irish abbeys. It was a Cistercian house founded by William the Earl Marshall in about 1200, in fulfilment of a vow he made when in danger of losing his life during a stormy crossing from England. The first monks came from Tintern in Monmouthshire.

The remains are later than the foundation date and many of the details, such as the east window and the buttresses with gablets, are strikingly like the same features in the church of the Monmouthshire parent house, built between 1269 and 1288. The Irish abbey, therefore, also belongs to the late 13th century. The Cistercian Rule forbade the building of large towers, but the massive central tower of Tintern Minor appears to be original and represents an early departure from Cistercian usage. Closer examination, however, reveals that this great tower was not primarily a belfry but a structural device. The pointed arches of the crossing rise above the tops of the nave walls; consequently the roofs could not run straight through to the chancel arch. With a tower over the crossing all the roofs could butt against its walls. The tower is as wide as the main body of the church and could not have been added later. Originally it was probably lower and assumed its present grand height only during the 15th century when the Cistercians had succumbed to the temptation to indulge in architectural display. The stepped crenellations of Tintern are of a type that crown Irish medieval buildings so frequently that they can be described as a distinctive and peculiar feature of Irish Gothic. Yet the motif did not originate in Ireland. It occurs in Catalonian monastic churches and in the French province of Roussillon in the Pyrenees.

After the Dissolution, the Abbey church was converted into a dwelling, where a descendant of the grantee is still living. The lay owners filled in some of the huge nave and transept windows, inserted Tudor mullioned lights, and built apartments on several floors. During the 18th century the south transept was given a neo-Gothic façade. The converted building is enclosed by the ruinous, yet massive, ivy-mantled walls of the original structure and is itself now only partially occupied and fast falling into decay.

27 CROSS OF THE SCRIPTURES, CLONMACNOIS, CO. OFFALY

Clonmacnois, the euphonious name of which means 'the meadow of the race of Nós', was, after Armagh, the foremost early monastic school in Ireland. As a centre of Irish art and literature it was unrivalled. Many kings of Tara and kings of Connacht were buried there, including Turloch Mór O'Conor and Ruari O'Conor, and in its heyday Clonmacnois was known as the 'University of the West'. It was a larger monastic city than Glendalough (plates 22–24), with workshops and the dwellings of workers and armed retainers as well as of monks. It is recorded that in 1179 no fewer than 105 of these houses were burned down. In its present ruined state Clonmacnois is one of the most poetic as well as one of the most spectacular relics of Early Christian Ireland. The remains, eight churches, two Round Towers, five High Crosses and more than five hundred early gravestones, many of them inscribed and decorated with reliefs, are superbly sited on high ground, vividly green, pastoral and solitary, overlooking the broad, glassy waters of the Shannon curving about a vast plain.

Clonmacnois was founded in the 6th century by St Ciaran. The saint came from Connacht and, according to a legend, King Diarmuid of Tara helped Ciaran with his own hands to build his first wooden church at Clonmacnois.

A worn inscription at the base of the Cross of the Scriptures indicates that it was set up for Flann, King of Munster, who died in 904. The subjects shown on this, the west face of the shaft, are *The Arrest of Christ in the Garden of Gethsemane*, *The Deposition* and *The Soldiers at the Tomb*. In the head of the Cross is the Crucifixion. The body is nude, the legs are bound, the spear-bearer stands on the left, the giver of drink on the right-hand side of Christ. This representation of the group is typical of the Irish sculptured crosses of the 10th century. The feeling of these simpler and more ample reliefs is less dramatic, less intense than the brilliantly organized and crowded panels on the Cross of Muiredach (plate 18).

28 ROUND TOWER IN THE CHURCHYARD OF ST BRIGID'S CATHEDRAL, KILDARE, CO. KILDARE

In ancient records the graceful, tapering stone towers, which are among the most striking features of pre-Norman Irish monasteries, are called *Cloigtheach* or 'Bell Houses'. They were indeed church belfries, but they were also used as watch towers and as places of refuge, very necessary at the time, between AD 850 and 1000, when pagan Norse pirates were harassing the Christian monasteries. The towers were built on a circular plan for the practical reason that it presented no corner stones which an enemy could prise out. The door, as here, was raised to a considerable height above the ground, beyond the reach of a battering ram, and without a ladder it was inaccessible. Inside the tower were four or five storeys with wooden floors. The bell was not, as in medieval and modern belfries, suspended, but rung by hand from the top storey; and whereas each of the lower storeys was lit by only one small window, the bell storey might boast four, six or even eight windows. The bellringer would ring the bell out of each window in turn. The tower at Kildare (106 feet high), which was part of St Brigid's monastery, has been much altered and renovated. The opening shown in the photograph is Romanesque and the original conical roof was replaced by a castellated parapet, probably early in the 19th century.

The monastery was founded by St Brigid (*see* note 48) in the 5th century and its church was the most important in the Kingdom of Leinster. It was remarkable in being a double monastery for both monks and nuns, ruled by an abbess and an abbot bishop. It is thought that St Brigid's foundation may have succeeded a pagan sanctuary, elements from the ritual of which were perpetuated in the Christian shrine. Until the Dissolution a sacred flame burnt ceaselessly there within a circular enclosure forbidden to men and attended by nineteen nuns.

The Tower was used as a fortress in 1641 and bombarded by the Confederate Catholic general, Lord Castlehaven.

29, 30 THE VILLAGE STREET AND BRIDGE, INISTIOGE, Co. KILKENNY

Inistioge resembles one of those planned English villages of the 18th and early 19th centuries like Milton Abbas or Wimpole, laid out by wealthy landowners to form part of a 'picturesque' landscaped terrain. Its whitewashed cottages, nearly all of the 18th century, are grouped about a lime-shaded green in a magnificently timbered setting on the banks of the Nore, and this sylvan scene is dominated by the ruins of a medieval priory (plate 31). The original little town was destroyed by the Cromwellians and largely rebuilt by Sir William Fownes. This ancestor of the Tighe family (*see* note 31) lived nearby at Woodstock House (destroyed in 1922), designed for him in 1735 by Francis Bindon. Bindon probably had a hand in planning the layout of the village; he was the architect of the grand ten-arched bridge over the Nore, the last bridge to span the river before it joins the Barrow at New Ross.

Fishing is one of the great sports of Ireland and traditional methods of fishing other than angling are still in use, although they have been made illegal. Poachers in the Nore use a staked net in the form of a conical trap for taking salmon, and trout are caught with a horsehair noose. The salmon spear, a three-pronged implement, is also still found in these regions. The fish are attracted at night by the burning of bog-fir splinters or lumps of turf soaked in oil.

31 THE PROTESTANT PARISH CHURCH AND RUINS OF THE PRIORY OF THE BLESSED VIRGIN AND ST COLUMBA, INISTIOGE, CO. KILKENNY

The present church consists of the chancel and central tower of the medieval priory founded *c.* 1206–10 by Thomas fitz Anthony, Anglo-Norman seneschal of Leinster, for Canons Regular of St Augustine. At the Dissolution the Priory was granted to the Butler family. It passed to Stephen Street in 1703 and in 1778 to the Tighes. Until the 19th century the Lady Chapel, now a ruin, served as a Protestant church. The tower at the west end of the present church is a typically 15th-century structure with the graceful stepped parapet so frequently encountered in Ireland (*see* plate 26). The massive north tower, known as the 'Black Castle', square-based with a rent and weed-encumbered octagonal upper storey, is now a Tighe mausoleum, containing an effigy by Flaxman of Mrs Mary Tighe (1772–1810), author of the narrative poem *Psyche*. This tower may date from the 13th century, for it was then that the Canons Regular were building towers at the north-west angles of the naves of their churches.

32 TOMB IN THE PRIORY OF ST JOHN, KILKENNY, CO. KILKENNY

The Priory was founded in 1200 by William Marshall, Earl of Pembroke, for Augustinian Canons. At the Dissolution the Priory was granted to the citizens of Kilkenny and in 1645 it became a Jesuit college, only to fall into the hands of the Cromwellians five years later. In 1780 most of the building was demolished to make room for a military barracks. The Lady Chapel of the Priory Church was restored in 1813 and became St John's Protestant Parish Church. All that now survives, apart from this, are the shattered chancel and fragments of the cloisters. Among the ruins of the sanctuary lies this crumbling tomb chest of a headless, footless, armoured knight and his lady, '....... Purcell and Joan, his Wife.' The style of the armour, the lady's headdress and the decoration of the sides of the tomb with ogee-arched niches and buttress-like pilasters indicates the late 15th century as the date of the monument. But the effigies and the tomb chest may not have belonged together originally.

33 'ISLAND VIEW', THE VALLEY OF THE NORE, CO. KILKENNY

In a country renowned for the beauty of its exquisitely clear rivers, as fresh and sparkling as Spenser's delightful descriptions of them written almost four centuries ago, the Nore is memorable, whether viewed from one of the numerous multi-arched bridges that punctuate its course, or from its steep, well-wooded banks. Seen from a height, as here, through an opening framed by larch, fir and the dizzy green of spring foliage, the river landscape – the shining stream, dotted with bosky islands winding into a moist, soft distance of smooth mountains and limpid sky – is extraordinarily like a Japanese painting. And the strange resemblance to the landscape of Japan is not peculiar to this scene; it is repeated again and again in every part of Ireland. It is possible that it was the recognition of this unlikely but striking affinity which led to the cult in Ireland, towards the end of the last century, of the Japanese garden. There is a small but ravishing example open to the public at Tully, near Kildare, planned to symbolize the Life of Man, and among private Japanese gardens in Ireland that at Ardna Sidh near Killorglin is outstanding for the way in which the natural features of a stark mountain scene, already strongly Japanese in feeling, have been incorporated in a minutely-contrived, utterly captivating oriental fantasy.

34 Dunbrody Abbey, Co. Wexford

Dunbrody Abbey is one of the most extensive medieval ruins in Ireland and one of the most profoundly moving. It lies on the east bank of the tidal River Barrow, weed-grown, abandoned – much as English ruined abbeys must have looked to 18th-century travellers in search of the picturesque. Sheep graze under the massive walls, wander into the undercroft of the shattered dorter or seek shelter in the chapter-house. The masonry at close quarters is silvery-grey and reddish, creating an effect at a little distance, against a background of sullen mountain and lowering cloud, of shining lilac.

The Abbey was a Cistercian foundation endowed by Henry de Montmorency for a colony of monks from St Mary's, Dublin, a daughter-house of Buildwas in Shropshire. The foundation grant was made in about 1174, but the building was probably not begun until the first decade of the 13th century. The bishop of Leighlin, who had been a Cistercian monk and is supposed to have supervised the building of the Abbey, was buried in the church in 1216.

The remains include a cruciform church of grand dimensions with six transept chapels, a central tower even more bulky than that of Tintern (*see* plate 26) and a large cloister garth with fragments of the sacristy, chapter-house, slype, dorter, calefactory, frater and kitchen in the usual order. There is no trace of the cellarium, which is generally found on the west side of a Cistercian cloister. The photograph shows the south side of the cloister garth from the outside, looking east along the walls of the frater and warming house towards the projecting end of the dorter, a huge room, 145 feet in length.

Founded at the height of a general movement towards austerity, Dunbrody is conspicuous for the starkness of its architecture, all the more impressive by contrast with its romantic setting and the irregularities in the masonry wrought by decay, weather and plant growth. The chancel of the church is, in accordance with Cistercian practice, straight-ended and pierced by three lancets. Both here and in the transepts the work is of the plainest; there is no hint of ornament beyond a chamfer or single roll moulding. The Cistercian Rule prohibited the erection of bell towers, but as time went on this restriction was ignored and some of the largest and most distinguished of surviving abbey towers are Cistercian. The central tower of Dunbrody, added in the 15th century, is extraordinarily powerful, though much battered. It has very small lights and the remains of stepped crenellations.

35 The Catholic Church, Kilsaran, Co. Louth

The church stands on the site of a preceptory of the Knights Templar. Catholic Emancipation was achieved in 1829 after two centuries of such oppression that no Catholic had been permitted to purchase freehold land or to inherit property, and no Catholic priest might be ordained. During that time those medieval churches which had not been taken over by the Protestant English had lapsed into ruin and the 19th century was therefore a period of great building activity. Ireland is particularly rich in Gothic Revival ecclesiastical architecture. Many churches of the 19th century, among them this delightful example at Kilsaran, preserve the gaiety and caprice which characterized the early Gothic Revival in England but which were soon crushed by the pedantic craving for accurate reproduction. The north, castellated porch of Kilsaran, with its toy-like tower of 1856 and boldly painted quoins, adds a note of fantasy to the plain rectangle of nave and chancel.

36 Shrine at Kilmacanoge, Co. Wicklow

No one can remain long in Ireland without becoming aware of the deep sense of the other-world, which dominates the imagination of the people to such a degree that the distinctions between dream and reality, aspiration and experience, cease to exist. In Ireland the gods are always at one's elbow, whistling in the air of the landscape immortalized by the great tales of Déirdre and Conchubar, Cúchulainn, Diarmuid and

Grainne, Oisin and Fionn, and brooding over the desolate, ruined churches and High Crosses of the Saints. It is the immanence of the supernatural in the Irish countryside which transfigures the sugary, commonplace imagery and humble materials of the countless wayside shrines and holy wells of our own day, so that we see them through a veil of poetry. The shrine at Kilmacanoge is a miniature Lourdes with a French inscription, a holy well and the coloured plaster figure of a woman praying to a plaster Virgin in a rough stone niche. Replicas of this group occur all over Southern Ireland. Nature has modified the original crudity of the figures, bleaching the colours of the painted robes, softening the folds with grey lichen, and clothing the stones with ferns; and the whole composition is ennobled by its wild and magnificent mountain setting.

37 A HOLY WELL NEAR DUNCANNON, CO. WEXFORD

Wells such as this, to which magical powers are ascribed, are conspicuous features of the Irish landscape. There are more than 3,000 holy wells in Ireland and their cult, like the worship of stones and the veneration of thorn trees (*see* note 81), is probably megalithic in origin. The presence of a holy well is in every case marked by a tree or bush covered with pieces of rag and fragments of clothing tied there by the devout so that the spring may take on their ailments or those of the persons for whom prayers are offered. Wells are believed to have the power to cure eye diseases, lameness, tooth-ache and barrenness. The special time for visiting a holy well is the first Sunday of each quarter of the Celtic year, the opening days of which fall in February, May, August and November.

38 SHOP FRONT, ROSCOMMON

The Irishman's preoccupation with the supernatural is illustrated by the presence of 'sacred objects' in the most prosaic and unlikely surroundings. The window in which the tawdry plaster figures of the Infant of Prague, the Virgin and Child and St Patrick, together with oleographs of the Sacred Heart, are the most conspicuous articles, actually belongs to a hardware shop. The robust Victorian lettering is typical of the bold decoration, redolent of the atmosphere of the last century, which is among the delights of the streets in all Irish towns.

39 SHRINE AT ST THERESA'S, BALLYSTORE, CO. WEXFORD

Although but roughly fashioned by the inhabitant of the cottage, with a figure of the Virgin such as might have come from the shop shown in plate 38, this shrine is an object of devotion, sanctified by the blessings granted in answer to the prayers offered up before it. The rags tied to the bush below the shrine testify to local belief in its supernatural powers. (*See* plate 37.)

40 KEYSTONE OF THE ARCH OF THE WESTERN DOORWAY OF KILLESHIN CHURCH, CO. LAOIS

This strange mask is characteristic of the Irish Romanesque style, which is remarkable for the concentration of design of outstanding quality upon the doorways of buildings otherwise invariably small and extremely simple. The head is carved with great delicacy in very shallow relief and the source of the stylization is clearly Celtic art. The keystone crowns a composition of four concentric arches carved with the most imaginative variations on the chevron motif, combining it with leaf patterns, Greek crosses, birds and animals and minute pellets that give the decoration the aspect of the finest repoussée work. The arches are supported by ornamental piers, the capitals of which are designed to produce a most unusual frieze-like effect of profile masks and intricate interlacements.

The date of Killeshin is unknown. Two worn inscriptions on the doorway would no doubt provide a clue but they have so far baffled all attempts to interpret them. It has been thought that they refer to Diarmuid, King of Leinster, who died in 1117, but this is no more than conjecture.

The church is in decay and the keystone head surveys a forgotten, overgrown graveyard and a rolling, pastoral panorama.

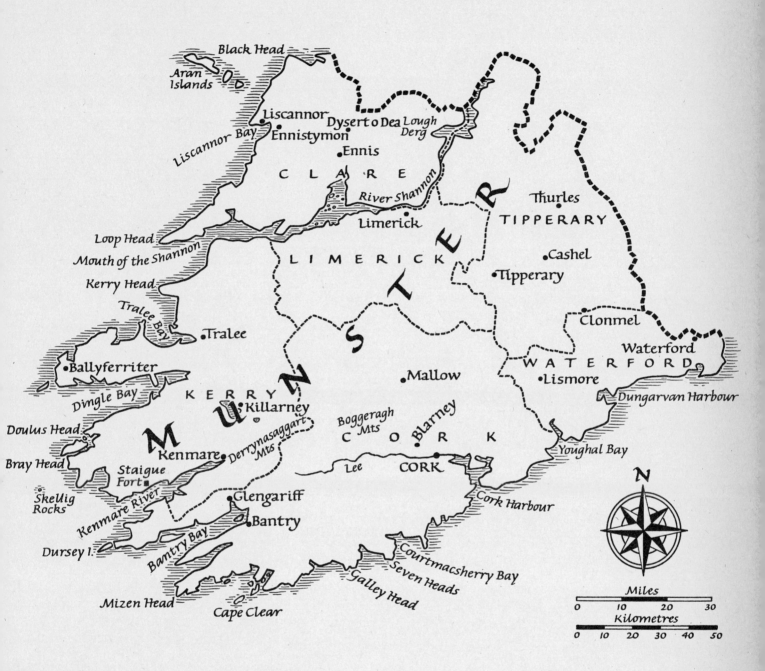

43

45

46

47

48

50

58

59

62

63

67

41 CORK AND THE RIVER LEE FROM ST PATRICK'S BRIDGE, CO. CORK

The spreading Lee that like an island fayre
Encloseth Corke with his divided flood.

Of the medieval Cork about which Spenser wrote, nothing survives and, though a few decayed Georgian terraces and the famous St Anne's Shandon (plate 42) remind us that a charming 18th-century town stood on this superb site, Cork is predominantly a 19th-century city. It has little of the architectural grace of Dublin and yet it is visually one of the most stimulating cities of western Europe. The difference in atmosphere between Cork and the capital is well conveyed by a comparison of this view of the southern arm of the Lee with that of the Liffey shown on plate 1. It is the difference between the romantic and the classical, the vertical and the horizontal, the painterly and the linear, the precise and the impressionistic. To look along the Liffey is still, despite the intrusion of a few functional cubes, like seeing an 18th-century aquatint come to life, whereas the city on the Lee resembles a Turner. Built on very irregular ground so that it is full of steep vistas, and embraced by the branching arms and tributaries of the Lee, Cork is transformed and dissolved by the Irish light glittering on water and on toppling terraces into a continually changing drama of chiaroscuro. The classical pedimented church on Pope's Quay to the right, is St Mary's, built by Kearns Deane in 1832–39. It is a Dominican church famous for its possession of a miracle-working 14th-century French ivory carving of the Virgin and Child.

St Patrick's Bridge, of limestone with mid-19th-century cast-iron lamp standards, was opened in 1859 to replace a bridge swept away in the Great Flood of Cork in 1853.

42 ST ANNE'S SHANDON, CORK, CO. CORK

The church stands on rising ground to the north of the Lee and the tower, with its pepper-pot lantern and dome crowned with a weather-vane in the form of a giant golden fish (symbolizing an important Cork industry, salmon-fishing), can be seen from all over the city. It was built by public subscription in 1722–26 to replace the medieval church of St Mary's which stood nearby and which had been destroyed when Cork was besieged in 1690 by Marlborough. The actual site of St Anne's was occupied by the remains of a church said to have been founded in 1199.

The fabric of the church is curious: the nave and lower part of the tower are of red sandstone, while the upper stages of the belfry are of glittering white limestone on the south and east sides and of red sandstone on the other two sides. The sandstone is reputed to have come from the ruins of Shandon Castle, the limestone from a Franciscan Priory on the North Mall. The bells, a peal of eight, were cast in Gloucester by Abel Rudhall in 1750. The tower almost blocks the narrow alley leading up to it, but the contrast between the silvery upper stages of the structure and the strong colour, not only of the base, but of the bars, shops and dwellings in the little street, counteracts the claustral effect of height and mass.

43 CORNMARKET STREET, CORK, CO. CORK

On the site of the first islanded settlement which marked the beginning of the city, and one of the few corners of Cork to preserve something of the atmosphere of the 18th-century town, Cornmarket Street is now the setting for an open air market. The church in the background, with its Ionic, pedimented portico crowned with a statue of the Virgin whose halo is outlined by coloured electric light bulbs, is the Dominican church seen on the right in plate 41. The Georgian shop-fronts and the façades above them offer an astonishing display of colour – orange, olive green, maroon, grey and cobalt.

44 CASHEL, CO. TIPPERARY

The famous Rock of Cashel, a steep and extraordinary outcrop of limestone, site of the ancient capital of Munster, rises from a vast, treeless, stony plain to dominate the little town. Unlike many Irish ruins, Cashel has been rescued from decay, and the weeds, nettles, piles of boulders and fragments of fallen masonry which enchanted travellers in the last century, have vanished. Yet the siting is so magnificent, the grouping of the bare, broken buildings against the passionate Irish sky so memorable that Cashel stands out as one of the most staggering visual experiences of Ireland.

A fortress was set up on the Rock as early as the 4th century by the Eóghanachta dynasts, who may have come from Wales. The Eóghanachta quickly gained control of all the most fertile lands of Munster; their principal ruler, the King of Cashel, automatically became King of Munster and knew no superior. It was not until 859 that Munster acknowledged the overlordship of the King of Tara. In AD 450 St Patrick visited Cashel and baptized King Aengus and his brothers. Four of the succeeding Kings of Cashel were either bishop, anchorite or abbot as well as secular ruler. Thus the connection of the Rock with the Church was early established.

After the death of Flaithbertach, abbot and king, in 944, Munster was overrun by the Norse invaders, who were defeated by Brian Ború in 963. In 977, Brian, the most famous king in early Irish history, was crowned King of Munster at Cashel. But Cashel was not the principal seat of Brian's descendants, the O'Briens of Thomond, and its political importance declined. In 1101, at a great assembly on the Rock, Muirchertach O'Brien granted Cashel to the Church and it became the see of the archbishopric of Munster. 'Cormac's Chapel', the most remarkable building in Ireland of its date, was founded by Bishop Cormac Mac Carthach, an Eóghanachta King of Desmond, and consecrated in 1134. A new and larger cathedral was begun in 1169 by Donal Mór O'Brien, King of Thomond; in the second half of the following century this building was swept away to make room for a yet grander edifice, the church whose ruins can be seen dominating the Rock in the photograph. The building was twice damaged by fire, once in 1495, and again in 1647. For the next forty years the Rock remained derelict. In 1686 the cathedral was restored as a Protestant church. It was again abandoned in 1749 and left to disintegrate until Cashel became a National Monument in 1874 and the ruins were tidied up.

The shattered cathedral of St Patrick, whose sturdy central tower figures so prominently in the photograph, was the work of three archbishops: Marianus O'Brien (1224–38), David MacKelly (1238–52) and David MacCarwill (d. 1298). It is a cruciform, aisleless structure with an unusually long eastern arm. The rent, truncated tower at the west end of the cathedral is all that stands of the archbishop's castle. By the north transept of the church rises a tall Round Tower, probably of the 10th century (invisible in the photograph), which testifies to the early existence of a religious community on the Rock. The gable flanked by two slender square towers, one of which is capped by a pyramidal roof, belong to the beautiful little Romanesque 'Cormac's Chapel'. Its plan is unique in Ireland, for the towers actually stand at the junction of nave and chancel and form little unequal transepts. The nave is corbel-roofed like

St Kevin's Church, Glendalough (plate 22), but the gable is remarkably high and the walls are arcaded. The Chapel is richly decorated and the ornament includes a feature rarely found in Ireland – the carved tympanum. There are two: one over the south and another over the north door. One shows a huge beast with a trefoil tail, while the other exhibits the strange image of a centaur shooting an arrow at a great lion who has just struck down two smaller beasts. The symbolism is uncertain, though the lion may stand for the powers of evil.

The two remaining monuments of importance on the Rock are the 12th-century Cross of St Patrick, of the same type as the Cross at Dysert O Dea (plate 57), and a large ruined building which once housed laymen or minor canons appointed to assist in chanting the cathedral services.

45 DETAIL OF THE FITZGERALD MONUMENT, CHRIST CHURCH CATHEDRAL, WATERFORD, CO. WATERFORD

Among a number of interesting monuments at the west end of Waterford Cathedral, the large memorial to Nicholas and John Fitzgerald by John van Nost, dated 1770, at once rivets the eye. It is a characteristic work by this master of the sepulchral tableau, a Fleming by birth who worked principally in England and Scotland. The draped, wonderfully plastic figure of Piety clasping the Scriptures leans on a medallion bearing the likenesses of the Fitzgerald brothers; beside them the winged figure of Time holds up an hourglass. The white marble, life-size figures are placed on a sarcophagus in front of a tapering slab of dusky grey marble.

46 INTERIOR OF CHRIST CHURCH CATHEDRAL, WATERFORD

The Cathedral stands on the site of a church built by the Danes in c. 1050, and rebuilt by the Normans. In 1773 a Committee appointed by the local council and supported by Dean Cutts Harman, urged by a desire for change and modernization which is only too well understood in the present age, decided to pull down the old church and erect a new one. It is impossible now to judge the extent of our loss, but the second half of the 18th century was fortunately one of the great creative periods and, although in a country where medieval architecture is represented largely by ruins the disappearance of any church which had escaped destruction in the 17th century must be regrettable, Christ Church is a rewarding and inventive exercise in the classical mode. It is no longer exactly as its designer, John Roberts, left it in 1779, for it was damaged by fire in 1818 and the fittings were altered by the architect Thomas Drew in 1891.

144

But the basic appearance of the nave is as Roberts conceived it. It is an unusually broad rectangle with an even broader pronaos. Its individuality derives from the handsome composite columns on their high bases of red marble, immediately reminiscent of the columns in Alberti's church of S. Francesco in Rimini, and the thick bands of naturalistic, coloured stucco leaves outlining the compartments of the vault.

47 A SHRINE AT ENNISKEANE, CO. CORK

The entire façade of a one-storeyed terrace cottage has here been turned into a shrine, built up round a small plaster figure of the Virgin in a miniature grotto in front of the window. This pious work is locally revered not only for its magic healing powers but as miraculous in origin, for the artist is not only old and infirm but almost totally blind. The decoration is executed in paint, wire-netting, plastic balls, beads, artificial flowers and living plants in a colour scheme of rich pink, deep ultramarine and white. Strings of beads on wayside shrines and by holy wells have the same significance as rags and bits of clothing: they represent the sufferings of the giver which he believes will be assumed by the sacred presence hovering about shrine or well. (*See also* plates 36 and 39.)

48 THE HOLY WELL OF ST BRIGID, LISCANNOR, CO. CLARE

St Brigid, one of the most popular of Irish saints, born a princess, founded the Abbey of Kildare in the time of St Patrick, the mid-5th century. The imagination of the people was perhaps stirred by St Brigid because of the similarity of her name to that of Bride, the chief female deity worshipped by the pagan Celts. St Brigid replaced her, rivalled the Madonna in the affections of the Christian Irish and became known as 'the Mary of the Gael'. The Holy Well at Liscannor is an important place of pilgrimage. It is approached by a damp stone passage, the stained walls of which are festooned with ivy. Along the walls are countless votive offerings each inscribed with the name of the grateful recipient of St Brigid's favours: sacred pictures and holy images – of St Brigid herself, St Joseph, the Virgin, St Francis, the Infant of Prague, St Anthony and the black-skinned St Martin de Porres (a particularly well-loved saint in Ireland) – bleeding hearts, statues of the popes and medallions. Several mouldering pairs of crutches testify to the virtue of the Saint and her well. There is not a single object of the slightest aesthetic value in the passage; these pictures and figures are so feeble and simpering that they cannot even be considered as 20th-century folk art. And yet it is impossible to approach the sacred waters without becoming aware of a strangely concentrated atmosphere of faith and devotion.

49 PLASTER STATUE OF ST BRIGID, ST BRIGID'S WELL, LISCANNOR, CO. CLARE

The entrance to the Holy Well (plate 48) is in a walled cicular enclosure below the Liscannor cemetery. Next to the Well is a hermit's cell, a late 19th- or early 20th-century structure on the site of a much earlier retreat. The centre of the enclosure is taken up by a flower-covered mound on which stand two painted, plaster figures of St Brigid in glass cases, identical except that one is life-size, the other no more than about three feet high. The larger statue was presented by Mrs Ann Healy at a date unspecified. The saint is holding a model of the Cathedral of Kildare (*see* note 28). Although mass-produced, this full-size figure of St Brigid in its glass box is sufficiently naturalistic to give a macabre and fascinating impression of life when it is first glimpsed.

50 TINKERS BY THE ROADSIDE NEAR ARDFINNAN, CO. TIPPERARY

Tinkers with their barrel-shaped caravans, sometimes no more than a handcart covered with a tarpaulin stretched across iron hoops, their piebald ponies and lean mongrels, are among the commonest sights of the Irish countryside. They are not to be confused with the gypsies or Romanies, for they are a Celtic people, descended from the wandering smiths of ancient Ireland. They still pursue their trade, calling at farmsteads to mend kettles and pots or, in return for a silver coin, to hammer out a pattern on a lid which then adorns the dresser and brings its owner life-long fortune. A little more ragged, a little more slovenly than the wildest and most bedraggled of the Irish, the tinkers speak a secret language derived from the Béarlagair na Sier, originally one of the high-caste languages of the priests of ancient Ireland. As the status of the wandering smiths declined, so Béarlagair na Sier declined too and it has now become a cover language used to conceal the subject of conversation from possible eavesdroppers.

51 GERAHIES, CO. CORK

The road which the rider is following runs along a narrow peninsula jutting out into Bantry Bay and terminating in the wild promontory of Sheep's Head. Far less known than the popular north side of Bantry Bay, this peninsula was until recently the scene of a community life which had scarcely changed since the Middle Ages. The donkey rider is carrying an archaic form of transport, a type of sled, known as a 'slipe', used for moving manure or turf, wrack, stones or potatoes. It can easily be dragged over rough, boulder-strewn hillsides or across bogs which are too steep or too sodden to take wheeled vehicles. A carrying frame such as this sometimes serves also for transporting the plough or the harrows from field to field. The slipe persists because for many purposes, in a terrain such as this, no better means of transport can be devised.

146

52 LISMORE CASTLE, CO. WATERFORD

The castle is one of the most picturesquely sited in Ireland. It stands on a steep, richly wooded cliff high above the broad smooth River Blackwater. Although the embattled, towered and turretted pile is almost entirely of the 19th century, the view of the castle from the opposite bank of the river is reminiscent of nothing so much as a brilliantly coloured late medieval miniature. In the rain-washed air the closely set, infinitely varied foliage, surging up to the pallid architecture, achieves a magic luminosity and precision which belong to Gothic painting rather than to reality.

The original castle, supposedly built on the site of the 7th-century monastery of St Carthach, destroyed by the Anglo-Normans in 1173, was the residence of the bishops of Lismore until it was granted in 1589 to Sir Walter Raleigh. In 1602 Raleigh sold the castle to Sir Richard Boyle, afterwards Earl of Cork and father of Robert Boyle the physicist, who was born at Lismore. The castle was restored by the Second Earl of Cork and, on the death of the Fourth Earl in 1753, it passed to Lady Charlotte Boyle, wife of the Fourth Duke of Devonshire. Late 18th-century pictures and engravings show the castle in a state approaching ruin, and early in the 19th century, in 1814, the Sixth Duke carried out extensive rebuilding and restoration. It was while this work was in progress that the *Book of Lismore*, an important collection of the Lives of Irish Saints and much secular material compiled by Aonghus O Callanáin, Friar O Buagácháin and other scribes in the 15th century for Finghin Mac Carthy Riabhach and his wife, Catherine Fitzgerald, was found hidden in one of the castle walls. It is known that in 1629 this manuscript was at Timoleague Friary, where Michel O Clery, one of the Four Masters, monkish authors of the celebrated 17th-century annals of Ireland, had recourse to it. The manner of its coming to Lismore remains a mystery.

When the castle was rebuilt, a Romanesque gateway from a 12th-century church at Reilig Mhuire was incorporated in the fabric, as were fragments of the bishops' castle.

53 BANTRY HOUSE, CO. CORK

Although less well known than most of the great Irish 18th-century country mansions, Bantry surpasses them all in its splendidly romantic site and the atmosphere of ruined magnificence which constitutes half the magic of Irish houses. The building stands on the edge of Bantry town, on an eminence overlooking the Bay where Whiddy Isle lies low on the water against the background of the Caha Mountains, smoothed by distance into the softest shapes of grey or violet. Immediately behind the house the demesne rises abruptly in a series of neglected terraces reached by precipitous flights of stone steps.

The central block of the house was built for Richard White, First Earl of Bantry, in about 1720. The wings were added in the same style during the following century. The fabric is of silvery brick with red brick Corinthian pilasters running the whole height of the building in the style of the mansion attributed to Thomas Archer at Chicheley in Buckinghamshire. The architect of Bantry is not known.

54 THE DINING ROOM, BANTRY HOUSE, CO. CORK

This sombre room is the most striking apartment in the mansion and one of the most haunting in any house in Ireland. It is typical that the effect should be produced by imitation as much as by genuine marvels and that decay should play a major part in evoking the unique atmosphere of this room. The colour, first of all, is as magnificent as it is unusual. The marble pillar in the foreground of the photograph is slate grey, the walls are indigo, flaking, fading and textured by damp stains. Round two sides of the room runs a spectacular, baroque, dusky-hued sideboard resting on curving lion legs. Cracks and chips reveal that the whole thing is of plaster, a reproduction of an Italian 17th-century bronze original. The pictures, in their billowing, garlanded gilt frames, are portraits of George III and Queen Charlotte, said to be by Alan Ramsey.

55 THE DEMESNE, BANTRY HOUSE, CO. CORK

On the north side of the house, a sweeping crescent of luxuriant uncut meadow grass flanked by trees goes down to a wooded slope and the shores of Bantry Bay. The demesne was laid out during the last century but there is now only the ghost of a formal design. Urns and the dazzlingly white statues of nymphs seem to rise casually, rather than according to plan, from the embrace of grass and copse. The statues are plaster replicas of French originals, some of them flaked and broken so that the armature is revealed, others half-submerged by the unchecked growth of bush and bramble. They stand on their high pedestals in an enchanted silence, frozen into attitudes of the dance above the ultramarine waters of the Bay.

56 DETAIL FROM THE SOUTH DOOR, DYSERT O DEA, CO. CLARE

A hermitage was founded on the site of the present ruins by St Tola, a bishop of Clonard, who died in 737. The remains of this 12th-century church have been recently reconstructed. The result is so far from satisfactory that the composition of the remark-able door now set in the south wall (probably the west door of the original church) is disturbed by unsightly inconsistencies such as the joining of two fragmented arches of

148

differing radii. The impact of the door is tremendous, nevertheless, not only because of the character of the sculpture but on account of its landscape setting and the vivid contrast it presents to the rest of the crumbling building, a rectangular structure as simple as the little churches of St Kevin at Glendalough and of St Columba at Kells (*see* plates 22 and 19). 'Dysert' means 'desert' and Dysert O Dea lies in a waste of bog and outcrops of pale limestone far from road or habitation; the munch of sheep and the wild cry of the curlew are the only sounds of life in the coarse-grassed fields surrounding and dividing church and High Cross (plate 57). The semicircle of intense, staring faces crowding about the richly moulded arch of the doorway is doubly impressive in such an atmosphere. The motif of the human head is common in Celtic art (*see* plate 40): it has seldom been used more effectively than here.

57 WEST FACE OF THE HIGH CROSS, DYSERT O DEA, CO. CLARE
This limestone cross belongs to the same period as that which is now preserved in St Kevin's Church, Glendalough (*see* plate 23) – the 12th century. The cross head is smaller than that of the early High Crosses, such as Muiredach at Monasterboice (plate 18); the wheel shape, as at Glendalough, has entirely vanished; and the figure carving, instead of showing scenes from the Scriptures, is limited on the main shaft to two subjects, the Crucified Christ and an ecclesiastic, here a bishop holding a crozier. The treatment of the Crucifixion is extremely stiff by comparison with the liveliness of the carving at Monasterboice, but the Christ is still beardless, as in early Christian art.

58 MUCKROSS 'ABBEY', CO. KERRY
The ruins of Muckross 'Abbey', or Friary, as it should be called, lie in a pastoral setting on the shores of Muckross Lake, below the Mangerton Mountains. The 15th century, when Muckross was founded, was in Ireland, as in England, a period when practically no new houses of monks of the older Orders were established, and when the friars, Dominicans or black friars, Franciscans or grey friars, the Augustinian and Carmelite, or white friars, captured the popular imagination with their preaching campaigns. But whereas in England the houses of friars are found chiefly in towns, in Ireland no less than forty friaries were established in remote country districts, chiefly in the south and the west. They were sometimes built close to the stronghold of a princely founder and protector; the seat of the founder of Muckross, Pallis Castle, was but a few miles distant from the Friary.

There is documentary evidence for the dating of Muckross: a Papal brief issued in

1468 grants indulgences to all who would visit the Friary and contribute to the completion of the building begun *twenty* years earlier. It was founded for Observantine Franciscans by Donald Mac Carthy Mór, whose tomb is in the ruined chancel.

Franciscan towers in Ireland are usually conspicuous for their slenderness, but the one at Muckross is almost as bulky as a Cistercian tower. It is as broad as the church itself, but of rectangular plan, much narrower in the east–west dimension. The plans of friaries differ in several respects from those of the earlier monastic houses, and the tower of Muckross illustrates one of the distinctive features of friary plans. It rises at a point a short distance eastward of the centre of the whole structure and is set on two walls pierced by narrow archways. The space between these supporting walls is spanned by small arches. The tower supports served to divide the choir of the brethren from the worshippers in the nave.

59 MUCKROSS LAKE, NEAR KILLARNEY, CO. KERRY

The Muckross Demesne, now the Bourn-Vincent Memorial Park, yields ravishing views of the Tomies, Shehy and Purple Mountains, which can be enjoyed from a seat in a jaunting car, an essentially Irish contraption, dating from the 19th century. It is a descendant of the wheel-car, a vehicle with much smaller wheels composed of three segments of wood dowelled together and shod with an iron hoop. The wheel-car was fitted with a platform, to which a box or basket was secured for the transport of goods, but which was covered with a straw mat to become a seat on social occasions. The passengers sat on each side, back to back, with their legs hanging down over the edge of the platform. Towards the end of the 18th century, the discomforts of this conveyance were lessened by the addition of wooden footrests. When large, spoked wheels took the place of solid wheels, and springs were introduced, the wheel-car became the jaunting car. One-horse cars were always preferred in Ireland to the four-wheeled vehicles which became popular in England and on the Continent, because they were so much better suited to the soft roads.

60 THE CLOISTER, MUCKROSS 'ABBEY', CO. KERRY

The cloister at Muckross lies, as is usual in Franciscan friaries, but in contrast to the general plan of monasteries of the older Orders, to the north of the church. It is extremely well preserved, small, and architecturally most interesting. The central space is almost completely filled by a giant yew tree, the mossy trunk of which is the colour of yellow plush against the pink and lilac stone of the arcades. Every tree in ancient and medieval Ireland had its particular uses, and the yew, which is often found growing in a monastic cloister garth, was reserved for the carving of croziers and shrines. The most extraordinary feature of the Muckross cloister is the structure of the piers: each pier is furnished with a buttress extension, sloping for the greater part of its height, then rising vertically to engage with the string course that crowns the arcades on all sides. The construction can be clearly seen in the photograph. Another peculiarity of the piers concerns the capitals and bases of the columns (two pairs to each opening): they are identically composed of three boldly projecting plain mouldings, so that they could be upended without altering the character of the cloister. The arches vary oddly in design. On the north and east sides (including the arches seen in the foreground of the photograph) they are bluntly pointed, while on the other two sides they are round.

Anyone familiar with the cloister plans of the other Orders will be surprised to find that at Muckross the first-floor rooms of the main ranges project over the cloister alleys, thus intensifying the confined atmosphere of the tiny garth. This is a typical practice in friary architecture, designed to give greater width to the upper rooms in the ranges.

61 CLOCHÁNS, FAHAN, DINGLE PENINSULA, CO. KERRY

'Twas Greeks and Phoenicians built these places. They made two parties of it, contending together as to who should have the better of it, and both were beaten by the Celts (that's the name for the Irish of those days). Then the Celts came to live here and that was the beginning of Irish history. And that is no lie.' This was the delightfully fantastic explanation given by the shepherd in the foreground of the photograph of the great clusters of beehive dwellings at Fahan. And yet there is a grain of truth in the fantasy, for the building technique exemplified by the clocháns, as they are called, the round plan and corbelled method, was known in the Mediterranean area and reached Ireland from there. The dwellings are scattered in countless numbers, singly and in groups, sometimes associated with forts, all over the savage promontory called Slea Head. Not a single tree redeems the stoniness of this vast deserted city of clocháns in their varying stages of decay. Only a few of these buildings have been examined by archaeologists and it is impossible to date them. The principle behind the structures, whereby courses of flat stones of a roughly uniform size are placed so that each course projects slightly further inwards as the building proceeds upwards (the roof being a continuation of the circular wall), and behind the design of the low opening, a lintelled door with sloping jambs, is found in the megalithic tombs of prehistoric times (*see* plate 17). But clocháns were still being built in the early Christian period and the modern outbuildings of little farmsteads on the Dingle Peninsula and all along the western seaboard (*see* plate 79) are constructed in exactly the same way. The clocháns closely resemble the corbelled farm buildings of Apulia and of parts of France, Spain and Portugal, just as the bleak landscape of these places resembles the treeless, stony waste of Slea Head. It is thought that when the clocháns were inhabited they were lined with clay, mud and sods.

Not all the clocháns at Fahan are circular. A few are rectangular in plan and are much like the Gallarus Oratory (plate 62). This great assemblage of primitive dwell-ings may have developed over different periods and some, at least, of the clocháns must be contemporary with the nearby Iron Age fort of Dunbeg (plate 63).

62 GALLARUS ORATORY, DINGLE PENINSULA, CO. KERRY

This far-famed building is the only perfect surviving example of a dry-stone walled Early Christian oratory on a rectangular plan. It was part of an eremitical monastery and is usually assumed to date from the 8th century. One of the great interests of this Early Christian church is that it represents the development of a native style un-influenced by Roman methods of building, for Ireland lay beyond the sphere of Roman invasion and Roman government. The Oratory, like the clocháns in its neighbourhood (plate 61), the chambers of the megalithic Passage Graves (plate 17) and some of the farm buildings in modern Ireland, Burgundy and Apulia, is constructed in the cor-belled manner (*see* note 61) without the aid of mortar. The stones of which it is built have been so carefully chosen, so ingeniously fitted together, that after the passage of about 1200 years the interior remains bone-dry. The workmanship is immensely super-ior to that of the clocháns. Some of the stones, indeed, are partially dressed. There are two openings in the church: the west door with inclined jambs and a double lintel, and a tiny round-headed east window. Shaped like an upturned boat or like a neatly stacked pile of turf, the Gallarus Oratory is wonderfully expressive of the stony waste in which it stands; a flat, eerie expanse swept by the Atlantic gales, half ringed by wild mountains, half encircled by a piercingly blue inlet of the sea.

63 THE PROMONTORY FORT OF DUNBEG, DINGLE PENINSULA, CO. KERRY

The number of prehistoric forts in Ireland runs into tens of thousands; they are the most widely distributed and the most numerous of any of the various categories of an-cient monuments. They are of several kinds: ring forts, hill forts and promontory forts. The promontory forts, of which Dunbeg is a spectacular example, were probably built at different times, but the structural features are similar to those of promontory forts in Cornwall and Brittany which are known to be of Iron Age date. Wherever the syllable *dún* occurs in a place name it indicates a large fort, especially a promontory fort. Dunbeg is stone-built and poised 500 feet above the sea on the edge of a sheer wall of dark, foam-lashed rock looking towards the whale-backs of the Blasket Islands. Part of the fort has fallen into the Atlantic. A fortified, dry-stone wall cuts off a triangular promontory and in this wall are chambers, the entrance to one of which is seen to the left in the photograph. They were shelters for sentries. Beneath the fort is a rock-cut souterrain, tunnels and chambers, the entrance to which is outside the stone rampart. Inside the fort, is the circular base of a very large clochán (*see* note 61).

64 THE UPPER LAKE, ABOVE KILLARNEY, CO. KERRY

The oriental aspect of much of the Irish landscape has already been remarked (*see* note 33). The resemblance strikes the imagination forcibly in the celebrated and stupendous panorama of the Killarney lakes from Dunloe Gap. The photograph shows the distant Upper Lake with its string of rocky islets, the shapes of which are defined by scribbles of fir trees, and the serrated ridges of the towering Macgillycuddy's Reeks. It is a landscape of convulsed mountains, giant rugged folds and deep valleys brightened by a chain of limpid waters, a landscape everywhere marked by precariously perched boulders, strangely rounded or startlingly jagged rocks, ice striae and corries – a terrain, in short, which is eloquent of the combined effects of erupting volcanoes and centuries-long glacial fretting, sharpening and smoothing.

65 THE CLIFFS OF MOHER, CO. CLARE

Perhaps the grandest and most awesome stretch of cliffs in Europe, these amazing walls of black, weed-stained rock rise sheer from a sea of terrifying violence to a height of well over 600 feet. They are of darkest sandstone.

66 THE BURREN, CO. CLARE

The terrain known as the Burren, which extends for about fifty square miles to the north and north-west of Lisdoonvarna, is one of the strangest, most primeval landscapes in Europe. Eerie and empty and uneventful, it inspires a sense of man's insignificance and of man's predicament more profound than that experienced in the face of the wildest cataract, the loftiest mountain or even an erupting volcano. It is a vast, bleached plateau of limestone, absolutely dry and treeless, shaped by millennia of driving rain and tempestuous winds into a series of mighty terraces and escarpments. Vertical joints show in the giant pavement, as precise as if they were part of a Gargantuan landscape design; and in these crevices grow not only exquisite starry mosses and wild thyme but plants which are otherwise found only in Alpine and Mediterranean climates: small, brilliant gentians and pale yellow and magenta Dryas. As the great plateau descends towards the sea, it disintegrates into huge boulders and the shore, pounded by the Altantic breakers, is littered with stones of nightmare size.

67 ENNISTYMON, CO. CLARE

The finely coloured village of Ennistymon is dramatically situated on high ground immediately above a series of admirably scenic cascades. It is exactly as though the water were sliding over a giant classical amphitheatre, for the bed of the River Cullenagh takes the shape here of a semicircle of rock miraculously cut into smooth regular tiers. The scene is as formal as one of Innes's stylized paintings of waterfalls.

68 THE RIVER SHANNON AND THOMOND'S BRIDGE: LOOKING ACROSS TO KING JOHN'S CASTLE, LIMERICK

The Thomond Bridge takes its name from the ancient kingdom of Thomond (East Co. Clare and later, for a time, all Clare and Limerick plus parts of Tipperary and Kerry) whose ruler King Mahon and his celebrated brother, Brian Ború, defeated the Norsemen, who had founded the citadel of Limerick, in the battle of Solohead in 967. The Thomond kings valued the town as a trading centre and Muirchertach Mór O'Brien, King of Munster (1086–1118) made Limerick his chief seat. Both bridge and Castle, according to the Elizabethan historian, Richard Stanihurst, were built by Prince John when he visited Ireland in 1185, though the existing structures show no evidence of anything of such an early date. Irish annals do, however, speak of a 'castle' at Limerick in 1202, and a record of 1216 states that the building was in need of repair. The Castle formed part of the walled defences of the town, commanding the approach from Thomond Bridge. It is a five-sided structure, the western and longest side of which (seen in the photograph) faces the river between two round towers. The left-hand one is the stronger and was originally the highest and most important of four towers in the angles of the fortress. All the towers were lowered to accommodate heavy artillery when barracks were built inside the Castle during the 18th century. The fortress is entered through a twin-towered gatehouse in Castle Street. The 15th-century tower visible to the left of the Castle is that of St Mary's Cathedral, originally founded by King Donal Mór O'Brien in 1176.

154

NOTES ON THE PLATES 69–84

69 DONKEY, WITH LOUGH GLENADE IN THE BACKGROUND, CO. LEITRIM

The lake, flanked by shelving, cliff-like mountains is the source of the River Bonet. The mournful braying of donkeys is as evocative of the spirit of the Irish landscape as the scent of turf fires; and these patient beasts of burden, marked with the sign of the Cross, seem to be as symbolical of Ireland as they are of Sicily and to provide yet another parallel between this far western island and Mediterranean lands. But in fact the donkey was unknown in Ireland before the 19th century. In an article in *The Proceedings of the Royal Irish Academy* (1916–17), entitled 'On the Introduction of the Ass as a Beast of Burden into Ireland', Professor Mahaffy remarks that the little donkey was conquering Hibernia when the Great Duke was subduing Iberia. The donkey came by way of Scotland to replace the Irish horses which were required in such large numbers in the Peninsular Wars; and very soon showed himself far more useful than packhorses in such places as soft bogs and slippery seashores. The donkey, laden with creels hung in pairs on a wooden 'straddle' or pack saddle, is one of the most frequently occurring sights in the west of Ireland; sometimes a whole convoy of animals thus burdened can be seen transporting turf, manure or sea-wrack.

70 WESTPORT, CO. MAYO

Westport is a planned town laid out in *c.* 1780 by James Wyatt, who was employed by the First Marquess of Sligo to complete and decorate Westport House (*see* plates 72 and 73). The little town is unexpectedly gracious and formal, set out around a hexagonal market-place and on both sides of a tree-shaded river running down to Clew

Bay. Wyatt's son, Benjamin Dean Wyatt, who also worked at Westport, made abortive designs, which can be seen in the House, for an enchanting theatre for the town. The trees along the river bank are chiefly sycamores; although these are not native to Ireland they are among the very few trees which can withstand the salt-laden gales of the west coast. The pony, once the universal draught animal in Ireland, is still much favoured. The one appearing in the photograph is attached to the characteristic flat cart (*see* plate IV).

71 DRUMCLIFF CHURCHYARD, CO. SLIGO

W.B. Yeats's grandfather was rector of Drumcliff and the poet's grave is in this Protestant churchyard. He died in the South of France in January 1939 and was buried at Roquebrune. Owing to the Second World War the body could not be moved to Drumcliff, as Yeats had wished, until 1948. The stone above his grave bears the last lines of the epitaph he himself wrote:

> *Under bare Ben Bulben's head*
> *In Drumcliffe churchyard Yeats is laid.*
> *An ancestor was rector there*
> *Long years ago, a church stands near,*
> *By the road an ancient cross,*
> *No marble, no conventional phrase;*
> *On limestone quarried near the spot*
> *By his command these words are cut:*
> *Cast a cold eye*
> *On life, on death.*
> *Horseman, pass by.*

The beautiful patterning of pale grey lichen on the tombstone in the foreground of the photograph (not that of Yeats, which takes the form of a harsh, ugly rectangle) is typical of the weathered limestone of the district and among the many visual delights owed to a damp climate. The valley beneath the slopes of Ben Bulben is the legendary country of Fionn and the Fianna and of Diarmuid and Grainne. It was on this mountain that Diarmuid met his death at the hands of Fionn. This was also the setting for Yeats's *The Mountain Tomb*, *Towards Break of Day* and *On a Political Prisoner*. It is the scene of the magical opening of *The Secret Rose*: 'One winter evening an old knight in rusted chain armour rode slowly along the woody southern slope of Ben Bulben, watching the sun go down in crimson clouds over the sea.' The poet's brother, Jack Butler

174

Yeats, was also inspired by this poetic landscape and the ghostly figures of Diarmuid and Grainne.

72 THE ENTRANCE HALL, WESTPORT HOUSE, CO. MAYO

As it stands today, Westport House is largely the creation of two architects, Richard Cassels, who first came to Ireland in 1728 to design Castle House, Co. Fermanagh, for Sir Gustavus Hume, and James Wyatt. The Palladian front of grey limestone is the finest part of Cassels's work of 1730 to survive. The interior has been greatly altered, but the entrance hall still retains the proportions and the most prominent features of the architect's design. The noble Doric frieze and the barrel vault are reminiscent of the library Cassels designed at Russborough, Co. Wicklow. A central court originally occupied the space now filled by the staircase of gleaming white Sicilian marble, and the staircase took the place of a library designed by Benjamin Dean Wyatt which went up in flames in 1826. The staircase was built for the Third Marquess of Sligo by George Wilkinson in 1857–59, when the horrors of the Famine, as keenly felt at Westport as anywhere, had abated. The marble *Angel of Welcome* in the niche was the work of C. T. Fuller in 1865. A further example of this artist's work, a seductive *Leda*, can be seen in the garden at Westport. The chandelier is Waterford glass of the 19th century. A most interesting artist, hardly known beyond the confines of Ireland, James Arthur O'Connor, who painted a series of ravishing landscapes of the surrounding countryside for the Second Marquess in 1818–20, is represented in the entrance hall by two arresting works, one of them showing the mysterious, mountain-locked terrain of Delphi and Lough Doo. O'Connor was a Wordsworthian romantic, one of the few landscape painters who have succeeded in conveying the sublimity of mountain and lake.

73 THE DINING ROOM, WESTPORT HOUSE, CO. MAYO

This is the most handsome room at Westport and one of the most severely elegant of Wyatt's decorative schemes. The stucco ornament may have been carried out by Michael Stapleton, with whom Wyatt was associated in Ireland. The treatment of the oval and circular medallions has a strong resemblance to Stapleton's work at Ardress House (*see* plates 107 and 108) in both subject-matter and border mouldings. Wyatt's rough sketches for the scheme are preserved at Westport. In the drawings the plaster-work is coloured sharp pea green and white, whereas the existing colours are grey, blue, gold and red.

The furniture in this room was designed for the Second Marquess by Gillow. On the table is part of a silver dinner service belonging to the owner of the first house on the site, Colonel John Browne, ancestor of the present Marquess. The marble chimney-piece in this room, not visible in the photograph, is a masterpiece of low relief showing delicately modelled classical figures harmonizing with the subjects of the stucco medallions. The sculptor was probably Flaxman.

74 THE INTERIOR OF A COTTAGE AT FALLDUFF, NEAR LOUISBURGH, CO. MAYO

When we cross the threshold of a traditional Irish cottage, we find ourselves standing on a hard mud or stone floor in the principal room, the kitchen. The cottage is only one room thick and small apartments may lead off the main room at either end, and occasionally there may be two attic rooms in the roof. This house follows the normal plan of three rooms. A bedroom opens from one end of the kitchen, while the room behind the chimney, the door to which can be seen in the photograph, leads into the 'parlour' or 'the room' as it is often called, reserved for family mementoes, for the dead awaiting burial, and for exceptional occasions. The most conspicuous feature of the kitchen is the turf fire. The fire is never allowed to go out and is the symbol of family continuity and of hospitality towards the stranger. In prehistoric houses and very early historic houses which have been excavated, the hearth was in the centre of the room and the smoke found its way out through a hole in the roof. A central fire with a chimney going up through the middle of the roof was not unknown even as late as the 19th century; Charles Lever, the novelist, describes one he saw in the Brannocks Islands. But the almost invariable position today is at the gable end or, as in this kitchen at Fallduff, against a partition wall; and this is, of course, due to the adoption of chimney flues. The area surrounding the hearth is paved even when the floor, as here, is of mud; and the fire burns at floor level and can be blown up by means of the wheel bellows. All the cooking is done on the turf fire, the basic pot being a three-legged cauldron known as the 'bastible', which makes an excellent oven. It differs remarkably little from late Bronze Age and medieval cooking pots, except that it is of cast iron.

The most important piece of furniture in the kitchen is the dresser and its position is determined by custom. It stands against the side wall, as in this cottage at Fallduff, or against the partition between kitchen and parlour or kitchen and bedroom. In the west of Ireland the traditional colours for the dresser are dark red and olive green. This essential piece of furniture is, however, seldom of good craftsmanship and never does it equal the Welsh or Lakeland dressers in quality. This may be due to the lack of timber in Ireland, it may be one of the results of recurring famine, or it may reflect a weak tradition in furniture-making among a people predominantly pastoral and indifferent to material well-being.

The table has only recently come to be considered a necessary part of the furnishing of an Irish homestead. Families were accustomed to sit round the fire at meal times with a shallow potato basket resting on the circle of knees. The tables seen in present-day cottages are always covered with shiny oilcloth boldly patterned with flowers or baskets of fruit. No Irish home is complete without its collection of sacred pictures and plaster statues.

Because the table plays a less important part in the Irish home than the hearth, the lamp (still an oil lamp in most homesteads) is not placed on the table but suspended over the hearth or placed on a bracket by a holy image. In this interior an electric torch hangs where the lamp is usually found.

75 TURF-CUTTING NEAR LEENANE, CO. GALWAY

This bog lies in a desolate, treeless region close to the Maamturk Mountains. The method of cutting turves in this deep, rich bog, in contrast to that followed in the bog shown in plate 25, is known as 'breasting'. The bog in this district is very soft and a broad flat breast blade is used instead of the winged slane (*see* note 25). It has a short handle, which is adjusted to the length of the worker's arm. With this implement it is necessary to make two separate cuts to detach a turf. The turves spread out round this Galway cutting are larger than normal on account of the extreme wetness of the bog, which means that greater allowance must be made for shrinkage. Turf usually shrinks to less than one-eighth of its original volume when dry.

76 ROUNDSTONE, CONNEMARA, CO. GALWAY

The Twelve Bens, the group of mountains seen across the harbour, dominate the wild, romantic region known as Connemara. It is named after Conmac (Conmaicne-Mara, or Maritima), a descendant of one of the sons of the fabulous Maeve, Queen of Connacht, and Fergus, ex-King of Ulster, whose posterity swarmed in the west. Properly speaking, Connemara is included within the barony of Ballynahinch, but the name is popularly applied to the region west of Galway town.

Roundstone is a fishing village on an arm of Bertraghboy Bay, an inlet of the sea running like a fjord far inland. The village was built *c.* 1820 by the Scottish engineer, Alexander Nimmo, and its swelling bow windows and sophisticated proportions are astonishing in their setting of bony rocks and scattered thatched homesteads. The harbour commands a view which is so overflowing with light that the whole dream-like landscape seems to be afloat. Although there could hardly be a more barren, stony terrain than this, it makes an impression of extraordinary serenity and silken smoothness. The glassy water, of the deepest blue and violet, mirrors rocky islets and sailing clouds with such clarity that the distinction between reflection and reality ceases to exist. The Irish name for Roundstone is Cloch na Rón, 'Rock of the Seals', and both names are appropriate, for the rounded, weed-covered rocks lying along the quiet shores are like the seals that bask on them and play about them.

77 AN OUTBUILDING, NEAR RECESS, CONNEMARA, CO. GALWAY

It would be impossible to give a date to this simple, shaggy little building which is so splendidly at one with its bleak mountain background. There is nothing, apart from the wooden door jambs (which could have been inserted at any time), to show whether it was erected a hundred, a thousand or only five years ago. The rough dry-stone walls are related to those of the clocháns illustrated in plate 61. But the roof here is 'flat' rather than corbelled. Horizontal beams span the breadth of the structure from wall to wall and carry a covering of loose material, such as old straw and turf, piled up into a more or less hipped form of roof and then roughly thatched with rushes. Such little outbuildings are usually placed alongside the low, one-storeyed homestead or stand in front of and parallel to it. They are used for a variety of purposes, as pig-sties, hen houses and storage places, primarily for fuel. The air blowing through the loosely packed stones helps to dry the turves. This primitive building is symbolic of the traditional way of life, embodied also in the story-telling, singing and the use of Irish speech which have all persisted here more strongly than anywhere in Ireland.

78 NEAR MAAM CROSS, CONNEMARA, CO. GALWAY

Carn Seefin and Leckavrea look down on this long, silent lake, one of the many shining stretches in this water-striped territory, which all form part of the great Lough Corrib. This is the heart of Joyce's Country, a district which includes the parish of Ross, that part of the parish of Cong which lies in Co. Galway and the country west of Lough Mask, and extends through the valley of Maam to Leenane. Roderick O'Flaherty, a 17th-century descendant of the chieftains of the west, one of the learned Irishmen of his day and author of a description of Connacht, writes thus of Joyce's Country: 'The half barony of Rosse, commonly called Joyce Country, from a Welch family of Yoes, Joas, or Shoyes, which held the land from the O'Flaherties (formerly part of *Partry-an-tselvy*, which extended from St Patrick's Hill in the Owles to Lough Orbsen) hath the barony of Ballynahinsy, Koelshaly Roe and the Owles to the west of it.' The Joyces were a Welsh colony who settled in the district named after them in the 13th century. Although the name is still common in that part of Ireland, the tribe has died out. They were fair men of huge stature. A memorable man of the name, known as Big White Jack Joyce of Leenane, is mentioned by Sir William Wilde.

Maam, a gap or pass, is a term of frequent application in Joyce's Country and Connemara.

79 A HOMESTEAD NEAR BALLINABOY, CO. GALWAY

Despite the inhospitable aspect of this boulder-strewn country it is surprisingly thickly populated, dotted with scattered homesteads, white and glittering like the limestone rocks which encompass them. The homestead in the photograph is a single-storeyed, rectangular, one-room-thick dwelling such as is found all over Ireland, but it also exhibits details which vary according to locality. The house has two doors, both in the kitchen, opposite to each other. Only the one in front is in general use. The back door (that seen in the photograph) is reserved for days when the wind 'blows contrairy'. The opposite doors were supposed to help regulate the draught for the turf fire before the introduction of chimney flues.

The gable ends rise above the thatch to protect it from the winds. The thatch has an undercoat of carefully dried and neatly placed sods, which acts as a warm blanket, and on this the straw is laid in prepared bundles. In some parts of Ireland the thatch is secured, as it usually is in England, by rods. Here it is held down along the ridge and at the eaves by rope pegged into the thatch. Two ropes, about a foot or two apart, stretched across the main slope of the roof and two diagonally placed ropes help to attach the thatch yet more firmly. The ropes are carried over the gable in rough steps left for that purpose, and fastened to pegs set in the wall. The thatch of this cottage is of oat-straw, which is readily obtainable although of poor quality.

Plate 77 showed a characteristic west of Ireland outbuilding. Two more are seen near this homestead, one in front of it and another beyond the chimney end. Both are constructed in the same manner as the little building near Recess, of rough dry-stone walling, but these resemble the prehistoric clocháns on Slea Head (plate 61) even more closely because the roofs are corbelled. The dry-stone walls which appear to meander erratically over the rough ground, enclosing the pocket-handkerchief fields near the cottage, are composed of huge stones cleared from the tiny patches of cultivated land. The larger stones are usually reserved for the upper part of a wall so as to secure the lower part with their weight.

80 KILLARY HARBOUR, LEENANE, CO. GALWAY

The harbour is at the head of an eight-mile-long fjord, the drowned valley of the Erriff River. It is utterly different in character from the lyrical, silvery expanse of water at Roundstone (plate 76). The rocky walls that rise steeply from the harbour's edge, the lower summits of the Mweelrea and Maamturk Mountains, which are seldom free from dark, smoky clouds, are the colour of lead blotched with sombre bottle green. They cast black shadows across the fjord and impart to the whole landscape an inescapable sense of menace. (*See* plate X.)

81 BALLYMACGIBBON CAIRN, CO. MAYO

The traveller along the road from Cong towards Headford passes through a bare, rather flat landscape, in which the most striking incidents are the silvery stones littering field and bog. Suddenly the stony theme assumes dramatic proportions: the Ballymac-gibbon Cairn – immense, glittering, looking as if it had gathered to itself all the stones of the district – towers above road and countryside, the most prominent feature in the great plain separating Cong from the distant Mayo and Galway Mountains. The Cairn is about 390 feet in circumference and is surrounded by a wall of rough boulders where thorn trees have taken root. The stones are said to cover a Passage Grave (*see* plates 16 and 17), but this remarkable monument has received scant attention from writers on the antiquities of Ireland. Oscar Wilde's father, Sir William Wilde, who built and owned Moytura House a few miles away from Ballymacgibbon Cairn and knew it well, describes it in his fascinating book, *Lough Corrib* (1867), and suggests that it is one of the monuments to the first day's fighting in the almost legendary Battle of Moytura between the Tuatha Dé Dánaan and the Fir Bolg. On this first day of the struggle, the Fir Bolg, who were later to be utterly crushed, had the best of it; to celebrate the event each warrior carried with him a stone for every man of the enemy he had slain, and it was supposedly from these stones that the Cairn rose. Wilde states that there was a large chamber within the Cairn.

The incident of the stone-throwing recalls the practice which still obtains in certain parts of Ireland, of throwing stones on cairns which form 'stations' when a pilgrimage

180

is made in honour of a saint, as at Glencolumbkille, Co. Donegal (*see* plate 100). Until recent times also it was the custom in Ireland for everyone who passed by the site of a violent death, whether murder, accident or suicide, to throw a stone on a pile commemorating the event. This stone-throwing, like so much in Ireland, has distinctly Mediterranean overtones: it strangely recalls the practice of Greek warriors who, when going into battle, would each fling down a stone on a pile. When the combat was over each survivor took a stone from the mound. The stones left behind commemorated and recorded the numbers of the slain.

The thorn trees which have rooted themselves about the Cairn have already been mentioned. Such trees are commonly found on ancient monuments such as this, or by holy wells, or scattered through the fields, and may be counted by the thousand. The Irish say that they were never planted but have sprung up of their own accord. Sometimes they are spoken of as 'gentry' thorns, an epithet often applied to the faeries. Thorn trees must never be uprooted and never lopped. Certain thorns are dedicated to Irish saints and when funerals pass that way the mourners place stones beside the thorn until a huge cairn is made. Such cairns line the roads to the graveyards of Aran.

82 IRON AGE STONE, CASTLESTRANGE, CO. ROSCOMMON
This granite cult stone with its spiral decoration, an Irish manifestation of La Tène of about 500 BC, which has no counterpart in Britain, and thus seems to suggest direct influence or even immigration from the mainland, lies like a giant egg in the decaying demesne of roofless, gutted Castlestrange near the River Suck. This La Tène phase of the Irish Iron Age has the strangest and most obvious affinities with the far earlier period of the art of New Grange (*see* plate 16).

83 CROAGH PATRICK FROM LECANVEY PIER, CO. MAYO
Quartz-veined Croagh Patrick is the Holy Mountain of Ireland. St Patrick is said to have fasted on the mountain top for forty days, and every year thousands of devout pilgrims climb shoeless to the summit before dawn on the last Sunday in July (Garland Sunday). Until the early 19th century the pilgrimage took place on Garland Friday. The ascent, from Murrisk, to the left of the photograph, is at first gentle and brings the pilgrim to the initial 'station' at the base of the mountain cone, Leacht Mhionnáin, where he makes seven praying circuits. From now on the climb is extremely arduous. The highest point is marked by a modern chapel on the site of an ancient structure and here further prayers are said, followed by fifteen praying circuits

round the chapel. The next 'station' is Leaba Phádraig, a pile of stones, where the pilgrim must make seven circuits; and the last 'station' is Reilg Mhuire, an enclosure with three stone mounds, round each of which the pilgrim must walk seven times. At the base of the cone is a deep hollow through which St Patrick is said to have driven the demon Carra right down to the foot of the mountain with such violence that water burst forth and formed Lough na Carra, the scene of George Moore's birth, of his novel *The Lake*, and the place where his ashes are scattered.

84 THE CHANCEL, BALLINTOBER ABBEY, CO. MAYO

The Abbey was founded in 1216 by Cathal Crovdearg O'Conor, King of Connacht, for Canons Regular of St Augustine, on the site of a Patrician monastery and near a well where, according to tradition, St Patrick baptized many converts. The abbey was completed and dedicated to the Holy Trinity before 1225. In the Middle Ages it was from Ballintober Abbey that pilgrims began their long journey on foot to Croagh Patrick (*see* plate 83).

When Ballintober was suppressed in 1542 the church was unroofed; it was still further savaged by the Cromwellians in 1653, and the lower tower over the crossing collapsed shortly afterwards. But despite its violent history and despite the destruction of the monastic buildings, Mass has been celebrated in the church of Ballintober Abbey without a single break from the time of its foundation until the present day.

The eastern parts of the 13th-century church, the chancel and the transepts, each with two chapels, survive, together with the partially restored walls of the roofless nave. This nave had been rebuilt after a fire in 1265. The chancel exhibits the characteristics of the Transitional style – round-headed and bluntly pointed arches and foliage-carved capitals – interpreted with striking originality. The general impression is of massive austerity, an impression conveyed principally by the colossal scale of the perfectly plain cross and groin-ribs. But this is belied by the surprising and contrasting delicacy of the clustered wall shafts and their leafy capitals, from which the giant ribs spring. These shafts illustrate another peculiar feature of far western Gothic – they do not start from the floor but rise from the wall at a point, about shoulder height, down to which the shafts taper.

The altar is the original 13th-century stone slab.

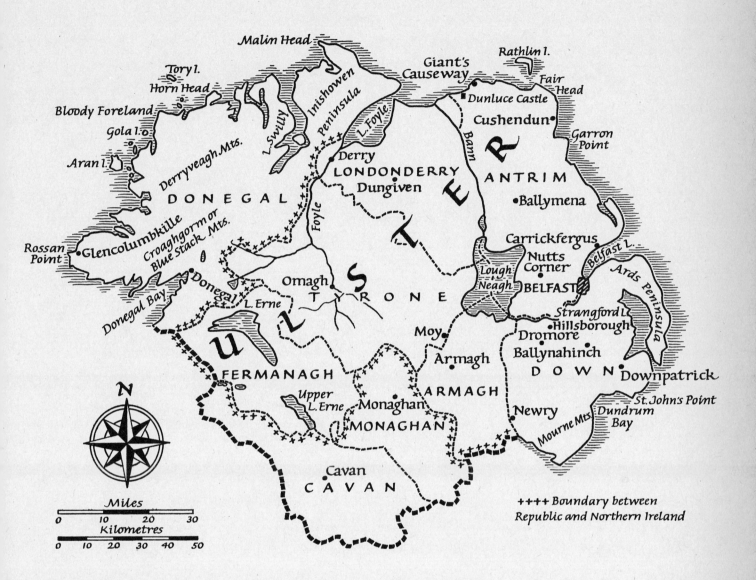

86

87

89

97

98

103

103

104

107

106

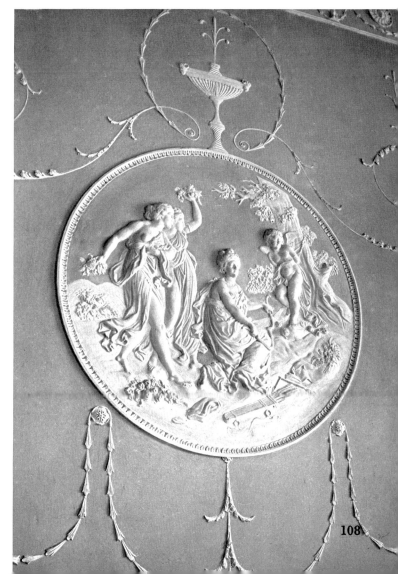

108

109

85 BELFAST DOCKS, CO. ANTRIM-CO. DOWN

The vast commercialized, manufacturing city of Belfast seems to have little connection with the essential Ireland. It is perhaps the only place in the whole country that felt the full, disastrous effects of the industrial revolution. Queen's Island, scene of the Docks and the world-famous shipbuilding yards of Harland and Wolff, catches the eye and imagination more than any other part of the Ulster capital. Cranes and gantries swing like giant mobiles against the cotton-wool sky, the air throbs with the sounds of drill and siren. Immense liners from Germany, Japan or Italy, and tankers from Russia, sharply recall the world beyond Ireland, a world which, roaring and rushing compulsively towards the 1980s and 90s, is utterly opposed to this slow, timeless land where customs and traditions are still observed and tools are still used which have been obliterated in every place where the machine flourishes.

86 THE PROTESTANT CHURCH, CHARLEMONT, CO. ARMAGH

The church stands so close to Moy or The Moy, as it is always called, that it seems to belong to that village rather than to Charlemont; and its architectural style has certainly been influenced by the distinctive character of Moy. That village, which was built at the expense of James Caulfield, Earl of Charlemont and Commander-in-Chief of the Irish Volunteers, was based on the plan of Marengo in Lombardy, and George Ensor, the Dublin architect (*see* note 106) designed some of the buildings in the Italianate piazza. The unknown nineteenth-century architect of the church has cleverly and amusingly adapted the Gothic Revival style to the classical character of Moy. A typically Italianate, pedimented façade and a strongly horizontal plan have been embellished with Gothic trappings, narrow lancets, one of them thrusting through the pediment, a battlemented, pinnacled porch and a pinnacled bell-cote.

87 THE SCREEN, LOOKING WEST, THE CATHEDRAL CHURCH OF THE HOLY TRINITY
OF DOWN, DOWNPATRICK, Co. DOWN

St Patrick is said to have founded a church on the site of this cathedral and his remains
are supposed to lie to the south of the present structure. But there is no mention of a
monastery of Down in Irish annals until 583, and knowledge of St Patrick's burial
place had been lost by the 9th century. The monastery was destroyed by an earthquake
in 1245, again demolished by Edward Bruce in 1315 and yet once more by English
forces in 1538. The church lay derelict until 1790 when the chancel was restored to
serve as a cathedral for the Protestant diocese of Down. It is to this first period of
restoration that the screen belongs, that period of the Gothic Revival when fantasy had
not yet been extinguished by the passion for correct detail. Like the little church at
The Moy, above, it combines the classic and Gothic modes. The gallery front projecting over the lower stage is typically Palladian, while the ogee arcading, the Tudor-
esque panelling of the stalls and the 'Early English' clustered columns are eloquent of
the early Gothic Revival.

88 THE PARISH CHURCH, HILLSBOROUGH, Co. DOWN

The town of Hillsborough was laid out for Wills Hill, First Earl of Hillsborough and
First Marquess of Downshire. There was already a church on the site – a restoration
undertaken by the Earl's ancestor, Arthur Hill, at the instigation of Jeremy Taylor
after the original church, erected by Peter Hill in 1636 had been ravaged by fire in 1641.
But the magnificent church designed for Wills Hill in 1773 completely effaced its
predecessors. The architect of this remarkable work has been scandalously forgotten,
though perhaps some record of his name may one day be found in the papers of the
Hill family. The town is built in the classical style, whereas the Gothic mode has
been chosen for the church. Although part of the structure is make-believe – the
vaulting, for instance, like that of all 18th-century Gothic buildings, is of plaster – the
plan is a serious and extremely interesting variation on the medieval cruciform design,
and a complete departure from the rectangular, classical theme. The plan is that of a
Greek cross with transepts occurring in the exact centre of the total length of the church.
Each of these transepts terminates, with striking originality, in a massive square tower,
so that, viewed from afar, the soaring western steeple is counterbalanced by the flanking
arms and immensely solid terminal towers of the transepts. Perhaps the germ for this
idea of the transept towers came from Cashel (*see* plate 44), where towers form rudi-

mentary transepts to Cormac's Chapel. The photograph shows a view towards the south transept through the 'Early English' tower arch. The Bishop's Throne on the right belongs to the same period as the church. At that time, the Cathedral of Down-patrick (plate 87) still lay in ruins and it was Wills Hill's intention that his church should become the Diocesan Cathedral.

89 THE CLASSICAL FAÇADE OF CASTLEWARD HOUSE FROM THE GROUNDS, CO. DOWN

Giant oaks and beeches frame the distant view of Castleward across the demesne which was landscaped in the 18th century for Bernard Ward, First Lord Bangor. The Castleward demesne had belonged to the Ward family since the second half of the 16th century. The original house on the site was improved and enlarged by Michael Ward, Lord Bangor's father, perhaps by Richard Cassels (*see* note 72). Mrs Delany stayed at the earlier house and described it in her letters as 'altogether one of the finest places I ever saw'. The house shown in the photograph was nearing completion in 1772. As with so many of the most interesting buildings in Ireland, the name of the architect is not known. But there appears to be nothing particularly exciting about this south-west front of Castleward. It is an accomplished but rather cold exercise in the Palladian style, with a boldly rusticated lower stage and a projecting central block with three arches surmounted by four Ionic columns and a pediment bearing the Ward arms. It is only when this noble but conventional composition is considered in relation to the north-east façade that the fascinating, unique character of Castleward is revealed. For that façade is all battlements and pointed windows. Gothic and classic are thus united under one roof. This totally unexpected and unparalleled arrangement is expressive of a disagreement between Lord Bangor and his wife, Lady Anne, over the choice of style for their new mansion. They eventually resolved to differ and she gave the north-east front its Gothic dress, while he imposed the Palladian manner on the south-west façade.

90 THE DEMESNE, CASTLEWARD, CO. DOWN

The demesne of Castleward slopes down from the house and yields through vistas of trees, like the wings on a stage, a view of melting recessions resembling those in a paint-ing by Claude – steps, balustraded terraces, the gleam of the calm water of Strangford Lough and long, shadowy hills. If the house is half Gothic, half classic, the creator of the demesne, like Claude, used the furniture of the classical mode in a design which is wholly romantic, almost intolerably nostalgic.

91 THE SITTING ROOM, CASTLEWARD, CO. DOWN

The disparity in taste which distinguishes the exterior of Castleward is also apparent throughout the interior. A classical hall (Lord Bangor's choice) leads into a Gothic saloon (Lady Bangor's preference). Dining room and music room are uncompromisingly classical, while in the sitting room Lady Anne's predilection for Gothic takes on grotesque proportions. Not even at Arbury are the fan vaults of such exaggerated, swollen aspect. Dwarfing, crushing all else, they create an atmosphere of nightmare. This is perhaps the most eccentric Georgian Gothic room in existence.

92 DUNLUCE CASTLE, CO. ANTRIM

No other rock-sited castle equals Dunluce for sheer romantic enchantment. Cylindrical towers, part of a curtain wall and a riot of Jacobean gables and chimneys crowd onto a solitary, sea-girt headland. The name suggests that the castle may have taken the place of a promontory fort (*see* plate and note 63); a rock-cut souterrain beneath the outer court, much older than the castle remains, supports this conclusion. Nothing, however, is known of its early history. Dunluce may have been built by Richard de Burgh, Earl of Ulster in about 1300, but there is no documentary evidence for this supposition which rests on local tradition. The ruins indicate that this first structure was rectangular with strong corner towers. The castle was held at different times by the McQuillans and the McDonnells, who altered and enlarged it. The gatehouse appears to be 16th-century work, and the ruins of a 16th- or 17th-century hall-house occupy the outer court. Some of the buildings in the second court may have been the quarters of the garrison when, for a short time in 1584, Lord-Deputy Perrott had ousted the McDonnells. In 1639 part of the domestic range fell into the sea together with a number of servants. After the end of the so-called Eleven Year's War in 1652 and the defeat by Cromwell of the Catholic-Royalist armies, the Earls of Antrim, descendants of the McDonnells, left the Castle and since then it has been slowly decaying.

93 CUSHENDUN, CO. ANTRIM

The photograph shows the ruined keep of Castle Carra where the legendary hero, Séan the Proud, is supposed to have been murdered by the McDonnells in 1567. The quintessential character of Irish ruin is embodied in this ivy-shrouded, featureless fragment of masonry on the remote north-east coast. The beauty of the remains strewn in such rich profusion all over the landscape is nearly always picturesquely desolate rather than architectural and nearly always associated with legend or folktale rather

212

than with recorded history. Rock-cut souterrains in the proximity of this ruin suggest, as in the case of Dunluce (plate 92), that the name Cushen-*dún* is connected with a promontory fort.

94 THE GIANT'S CAUSEWAY, CO. ANTRIM

This exotically formed and celebrated series of cliffs is the result of repeated gigantic outpourings of volcanic basalt in Tertiary times, which cooled into the shapes of a lower layer of thousands upon thousands of regular hexagonal columns and an upper layer of thin irregular prisms that look like the wildest architectural fantasies. The overwhelming scale of this vast conglomeration of petrified crystals is conveyed by the figure of the nun.

95 BISHOP GATE AND THE CITY WALL, LONDONDERRY, CO. DERRY

Derry, called Londonderry from its association with the city of London, was granted by James I to the citizens of the capital of England, who surrounded it with tremendously thick walls and bastions and planted it with Protestant settlers. The walls, pierced by four gates, and the bastions are all that survive from the original plantation, though the plan of the town within the enclosure, a roughly rectangular grid with a square (the Diamond), is still clear. Bishop Gate is not the original structure; it was rebuilt to the design of Aaron Baker in 1789 in the form of a triumphal arch commemorating the epic siege of Londonderry (1688/9). It was the Rev. George Walker, rector of Donaghmore, who brought about the siege by persuading the citizens and garrison to expel the Governor and refuse admission to a Jacobite garrison. The trophies of arms and the laurel-wreathed head on the keystone of this otherwise austere design were carved by Edward Smyth (*see also* plates 5, 10 and 12).

By the early 19th century Derry had expanded beyond the 17th-century walls. The photograph shows the view from the old town through the arch.

96 ST COLUMBA'S WELLS, LONDONDERRY, CO. DERRY

The first streets to be laid out beyond the walls of Derry were as elegant as anything in Dublin – tall, plain façades with decoration confined to doorcase and fanlight. During the middle years of the last century, however, Derry became one of the chief ports for the emigration of those who sought escape from the horrors of the Potato Famine. One of the results of so much coming and going was that a considerable body of Catholic workers from the South found employment in the newly established shirt and collar manufactories, and settled in an area next to the quiet Georgian streets. Creating an environment which was entirely opposed to that of sober Protestant Derry, they lived in a maze of small-scale streets, in which many of the houses were one-storeyed, like the country homesteads they had left behind them. An enormous and imposing Catholic cathedral was built for these people in 1851. The little slummy streets pulsate with southern warmth and vitality. Walls are painted pea-green, maroon and cobalt; Gaelic script appears over some of the shop windows; and seasonal and church festivals are celebrated as in southern Ireland. The flags gaily fluttering across the alley in the photograph have been hung up in honour of St Columba, whose day falls on 15th June. St Columba, or Columbkille (*see also* notes 19 and 100), founded a monastery on the site of Derry in 546. By the 12th century it had become so important that it replaced Kells as the chief of the Columban monasteries.

97 COTTAGES AT GLENCOLUMBKILLE, CO. DONEGAL

The pegged and roped method of thatching, which is distributed all along the north and west coasts of Ireland (*see* plate 79), assumes a special and extraordinarily attractive form in Donegal. The roofs here are rounded, the better to withstand the terrible gales to which they are exposed, and this rounded form is achieved by breaking the angle of the ridge with short cross-pieces. The straw thatch is secured by ropes running both vertically and horizontally to make a complete network over the roof, and the ropes are fastened to the walls by means of rows of pegs below the eaves and round the gables. Another and older method of securing the vertical ropes is to tie the ends to small boulders which hang down over the eaves and keep the ropes taut. A close mesh of rope like that which nets the thatch in the foreground of the photograph needs more than a mile's length of roping. The rope, which is now generally of sisal bought ready-made, was formerly made of the tough fibres of bog-fir roots. In Donegal the gable ends do not rise above the thatch as in the cottage shown in plate 79, and the transition from roof to gable is often made smoother by plastering the stone wall with mud and lime-washing it.

98 THE 'SAINT'S TOMB', BANAGHER, DUNGIVEN, CO. DERRY

It is the contrast between the small size of this building (10 x 5 feet) and the massive stones of walls and roof, fitted together with such remarkable accuracy, which makes this oratory so exciting an object on its wooded knoll above the River Roe. St Muiredach O'Heney is said to have founded a church here in the 11th century and according to tradition is buried in the 'tomb'. The Banagher oratory shows a peculiarity of Irish church building which occurs in many early examples: the strange pilaster-like projections of the side walls beyond the gables. They may have served for the support of roof timbers in advance of the gable, but no accepted theory has yet been put forward to explain them. Here they support slabs of stone which follow the line of the gable and themselves support a projecting architrave. The crude, yet monumental, niche thus formed shelters a large carved upright slab, possibly representing an ecclesiastic, which looks as though it might once have been part of a cross.

99 DONEGAL CASTLE, CO. DONEGAL

The impressive ruins of Donegal Castle near the Diamond (or market place) are the remains of a great fortress transformed into a gabled manor house in the English style. A strong thick tower was built by the O'Donnells, Kings of Tír Chonaill, in the 16th century. The lower part of this structure formed the nucleus of the house built in 1610 by the English grantee Sir Basil Brooke. He added a gabled wing, inserted mullioned windows of many lights into the tower, and adorned the tower itself with four curious square corner turrets, one of which survives entire. The photograph shows the main room in the tower, the former banqueting hall with its ornate Jacobean chimney-piece, ornamented with heraldic devices, swags and scrolls. Above it, once forming part of a room on the next floor, can be seen a Tudor fireplace with a four-centred arch, a relic of the O'Donnell building.

100 GLENCOLUMBKILLE, CO. DONEGAL

This tranquil valley, close to the sea, though the water cannot be seen as the land rises sharply towards its edge, takes its name from the great St Columbkille (also known as Colum and Columba) of Derry and Iona who, according to legend, fought on this spot with demons who had escaped from St Patrick on Croagh Patrick (*see* plate 83). St Columbkille soon bested them and drove them into the sea. On the Saint's day, 15 June, a three-mile long *turas*, or pilgrimage, is made at Glencolumbkille, during which religious exercises are performed at fifteen cairns or penitentiary stations, most of them marked by the stumps of ancient stone pillars. These cairns were formed by the practice of each pilgrim throwing a stone on the pile in honour of the Saint (*see also* note 81). The great pillar shown in the photograph is the only one to survive entire.

Such pillars were simply sepulchral, or were set up to mark sacred spots; they were often prominent features of early monasteries. Later they were elaborated into full cruciform slabs. This pillar at Glencolumbkille is decorated with incised designs based on the Maltese Cross motif.

101 GRIANÁN OF AILECH, Co. DONEGAL

This stupendous stone hill fort, $77^1/_2$ feet in diameter and 17 feet high, a characteristic example of this most impressive class of fort, as distinct from the ring fort and the promontory fort (*see* plate 63), encircles the summit of Grianán Mountain and commands a wide, magnificent prospect of lake and hill. The entrance to this high ramparted fort is through a lintelled doorway, whereas less ambitious forts are approached merely through a gap in the wall. The structure has not been excavated and its date is unknown. It may go back to the Iron Age, as it is said to do in the *Annals of the Kingdom of Ireland* by the Four Masters. There are three outer fortifications which may be of earlier date than the central fort. From the 5th until the 12th century, it was occupied by the northern Uí Néill (Donegal dynasts descended from Niall Nine Hostager of Tara). The southern Uí Néill, led by Finechta the Festive, attacked and wrecked the fortress in 676; and in 1101, though it had by that time ceased to have any but a symbolical significance, it was despoiled by Muirchertach O'Brien, King of Munster, each of O'Brien's men being instructed to carry away one stone of the fortress. The fort was restored in 1870.

102 THE INTERIOR OF GRIANÁN OF AILECH, Co. DONEGAL

The enclosing wall of the fortress, more than thirteen feet thick at the base, contains guard chambers and galleries, and on the inside it is terraced. Steps, shown in the photograph, give access to the terraces and to the wall top for purposes of defence. In the centre of the enclosure were formerly the remains of a rectangular building. The terraced wall looks down on the beautiful lakes of Foyle and Swilly.

103 THE SALOON, CASTLECOOLE, Co. FERMANAGH

The circular saloon is the richest of those restrained rooms at Castlecoole which remain as the architect James Wyatt planned them. The elegant plasterwork is by Joseph Rose, one of the most highly esteemed of Adam's collaborators; and the black, grey and white scagliola pilasters were the work of Domenico Bartoli, probably a relative of Giuseppe Bartoli who was employed to make the scagliola pillars at Kedleston Hall, Derbyshire. The plaster Corinthian capitals were sent from London in 1795.

216

104 STOVE IN THE FIRST FLOOR LOBBY, CASTLECOOLE, CO. FERMANAGH

The graceful apartment, in the purest Attic style, which serves the first floor bedrooms at Castlecoole is one of Wyatt's most inspired designs. It is lit by a dome and surrounded by a gallery, the ceiling of which is supported by coupled columns. The four stoves which heat the room are set in semicircular niches above floor level and take the unlikely form of fat, garlanded pedestals surmounted by casts of Greek poets from the antique.

105 CASTLECOOLE, CO. FERMANAGH

The composition of Castlecoole, a central pedimented block flanked by colonnades with small terminal pavilions, was common enough during the last half of the 18th century, but the proportions here are exquisitely adjusted. The severity and simplicity of the Doric arcade are precisely counterbalanced by the weight of the balustraded parapet and the Palladian windows of the pavilions; and the white stone house is perfectly attuned to the verdant landscape, in which it is so closely set that a flower-starred meadow waves beneath its very walls. Castlecoole lives in the memory as one of the most poetically conceived of all the great Georgian houses of Ireland. The house is built of Portland stone, which was brought at fantastic cost from England, first to the port of Ballyshannon, then overland by bullock cart to Lough Erne and thence by water again to Enniskillen.

Castlecoole stands on the site of a fortified house which was burnt down in 1641. John Corry, ancestor of the present inhabitant, Lord Belmore, bought the demesne in 1656 and restored the castle. It was again destroyed by fire in 1689, with intent, to prevent it from falling into the hands of King James's troops. A Queen Anne house rose from the ruins in 1709 and the great avenue of oaks which led up to it still exists. But this house too went up in flames in 1787. It was Armor Lowry-Corry, who succeeded to Castlecoole in 1779 and who was later created Earl of Belmore, who commissioned Wyatt to design the present mansion. Lord Belmore himself acted as contractor, hiring the workmen and providing the materials. All the accounts for the building have survived and from them we learn the name of the principal stonecutter, William Kane. The work was begun in 1788 and completed by 1798. It is not known whether Wyatt himself supervised the work, but the architect who worked under him, Alexander Stewart, arrived at Castlecoole in the early summer of 1788.

106 THE GARDEN FRONT, ARDRESS HOUSE, CO. ARMAGH

Ardress House became the home of the architect George Ensor after he had married the heiress to the property, Sarah Clarke, in 1760. It was about ten years after this date that Ensor set about remodelling the house, which was a mid-17th-century manor built after an earlier dwelling had been destroyed in the Civil War.

With its steeply pitched roof and gables, the garden front of Ardress still wears something of the aspect of a 17th-century house, though the window openings and the curved screen walls, embellished with niches and recessed panels, are typical expressions of Georgian taste. The urn on the terrace is of Coade stone (the artificial stone made by a secret process at Mrs Coade's works in Lambeth and much used by Adam and his school) and dated 1790.

107 THE DRAWING ROOM, ARDRESS HOUSE, CO. ARMAGH

This, the most important room at Ardress, was the kitchen of the 17th-century house, completely remodelled by George Ensor. The elegant room is remarkable chiefly for its stucco decoration, the work of Michael Stapleton. The style derives from that of Robert Adam, but is still informed with something of the exuberance of the earlier school of Irish stuccoists exemplified in the decoration of 56 St Stephen's Green, Dublin (*see* note 2). The ceiling is patterned with circles, semicircles and segments of circles, outlined by delicate husk chains and reeding and enclosing urns and branching, spiralling foliage. The frieze, with its modillion cornice, consists of roundels set between standing *putti* holding fragile swags. The walls are ornamented with oval and circular plaques, festooned with husk chains describing loops and circles and ending in small medallions. Similar patterns occur in a number of Dublin houses decorated by Stapleton; drawings for those and for the Ardress plasterwork are preserved in the National Library, Dublin. The colours of the walls were once green and white, while the ceiling was white and grey. The drawing room chimney-piece, designed by George Ensor, can just be glimpsed in the photograph; it has inlaid, striped Doric columns and a bold frieze inlaid with Greek key pattern.

108 DETAIL OF MICHAEL STAPLETON'S STUCCO DECORATION IN THE DRAWING ROOM, ARDRESS HOUSE, CO. ARMAGH

This medallion, the subject of which is *Cupid Bound*, shows the vigorous modelling which is characteristic of Michael Stapleton's work, while the animated composition and the naturalism of the tree and foliage recall the brilliant, agitated rococo work of the Irish stuccoists of the two preceding decades. It is perhaps significant that Stapleton, who came of a Kilkenny family of decorators and was employed in Dublin in the

218

70s, was a friend of Robert West, the outstanding master of the great period of Irish plaster decoration, and that he was West's sole executor when the stuccoist died in 1790.

109 THE MALL, ARMAGH, CO. ARMAGH

Armagh was the birthplace of Francis Johnston (*see* notes 12 and 13), and the wonderfully preserved Mall, terminating in the classical County Courthouse, was designed by him in 1809. Terrace and Courthouse were planned as a harmonious group and the terrace façades are conceived as a single unit. The Mall differs from the Georgian terraces of Dublin (*see* plate 4) in both material and composition: stone takes the place of brick and the wall is no longer so severely plain or so sharply cliff-like. The ground floor windows are rusticated; a string course divides this floor from the two upper storeys; and a projecting cornice further emphasizes the horizontality of the design. Cast-iron balconies, curving railings and broad sweeps of steps leading up to identical pilastered, round-headed doorways, each with a fanlight like a sunflower cut in half, add rhythm, movement and lightness to the terrace.

110 ST PATRICK'S CATHOLIC CHURCH, ARMAGH

The town of Armagh preserves in its name the memory of the goddess Macha (*see* note 111). It was also the seat of the pre-Christian Ulster kings and was chosen by St Patrick as the site of his principal church. It is, however, the present Protestant Cathedral which stands on the traditional site of St Patrick's foundation. The Catholic Church confronts it from a rival hilltop, soaring up at the summit of a noble crescendo of steps. This imposing twin-towered pile was begun in 1840, but work was brought to a standstill by the Great Famine. The building was completed only in 1873. It was originally designed by Thomas J. Duff of Newry in the Perpendicular style, with a central tower in addition to the two western spires. The 'Decorated' church which was eventually built was the work of J. J. McCarthy, known as 'the Irish Pugin'. The decoration of the interior was entrusted to Italian craftsmen, who covered the walls with mosaics, among them medallions of the saints of Ireland, and used marble exclusively for the furnishings. The building is a powerful example of Gothic Revival art.

111 CARVING IN THE VESTRY OF ST PATRICK'S PROTESTANT CATHEDRAL, ARMAGH

This obese, intensely powerful, vital and aggressive, caryatid-like figure is one of several which were removed from the interior of the Cathedral, a medieval foundation, when it was restored by the English architect, Lewis Cottingham, in 1834. The earliest parts of the present building date from the 13th century, but there was an older church with a monastic enclosure on the site, the foundation of which is ascribed to St Patrick himself. This carving and its companions are probably relics of a vanished building. The head of this figure, with its close-fitting cap and rope-moulded eyebrows, is a coarser, more dynamic version of the type found at Dysert O Dea (plate 56), but it is nearer to the heads of the Gorgon on the metopes from Selinunte in Sicily than to anything in Christian sculpture. Armagh (Ard Macha) was sacred to the great warrior goddess, Macha, in prehistoric Ireland and the feeling behind this carving as well as the bow the figure is holding behind his head suggest lingering pagan traditions.

112 STONE FIGURES, BOA ISLAND, LOUGH ERNE, CO. FERMANAGH

On both Boa and Lustymore, two islands of Lough Erne, the traveller is confronted by stone idols, haunting triangular-shaped heads set on neckless torsos with rudimentary arms crossed on their breasts, peering above fern and flower. Some of the figures are two-faced, Janus-like. They were carved out of slabs of the living rock in the Christian era (in the 7th century, it is thought), but they speak eloquently of a far earlier iconographical tradition and of pagan worship and ritual. R. A. S. Macallister (*The Archaeology of Ireland*, 1949) believes the tradition represented by these enigmatical figures to be that of the Iberian Bronze Age fiddle-shaped torso idols found round the shores of the Mediterranean from Spain to Crete.

113 DEVENISH ISLE, LOUGH ERNE, CO. FERMANAGH

Devenish or Ox Island, in the great lake of Lough Erne, is one of the most exquisitely mournful spots in Ireland, for here the message reiterated again and again by the crumbling masonry all over the country of the evanescence of all human endeavour, achieves a peculiar intensity. The whole island is given up to ruin, and the impact of the shattered, roofless walls and scattered stones is powerfully enhanced by the contrasting perfection of the Round Tower, from the richly sculptured cornice of which four majestic heads look down on the scene of decay. The Tower is the best-preserved in Ireland and the most elaborately constructed, for every stone has been carefully dressed. In the 19th century an elder tree rooted itself in the conical cap and in 1834 this tree was blown down, carrying a great part of the cone with it. It was rebuilt in 1835 by one Robert Rexter, who has left his inscription on a stone under the cornice.

The Tower was part of an early monastery founded in the 6th century by Molaise, one of many Irish saints of this name. The remains of the tiny oratory named after the founder-saint belong to a later date than similar buildings at Glendalough (plate 22) and Kells (plate 19). The Cyclopean stonework of the thick walls seems to indicate an early date, but drawings made in the 18th century of the window and roof, when the structure was less ruinous, show Romanesque details similar to those of the cornice of the Round Tower and the oratory either belongs altogether to the late 11th or the early 12th century, or it was much renovated at that time. The tapering form of the Round Tower is confronted across a stony waste by the square tower of the 15th-century church of the house of Canons Regular of St Augustine, established on Devenish Isle in the 14th century as a daughter-house of the Augustinian monastery at Clogher. The 15th-century towers of this Order tend to be rather low and, as here, curiously narrow in relation to the width of the church. The supporting arches of the tower spring from curious tongue-shaped corbels, which appear to be peculiar to Ireland.

The greater part of the records and the portable antiquities of Devenish have perished, some in fires that destroyed the monastic buildings in 1157 and again in 1360, and many more in 1602 when the Abbey was occupied by English soldiers. A metal reliquary of the 11th century, the Soiscél Molaise, now in the National Museum, Dublin, was made in the Devenish monastery. It is about 6 inches high and adorned with interlacings and symbolical representations of the Evangelists and an Irish cross, and once contained a copy of the Gospels said to have been written for Molaise. This is the sole relic of a once richly furnished monastic settlement.

INDEX

Numbers in italics refer to the plates, roman numerals to colour plates

222